Everyday Mysticism

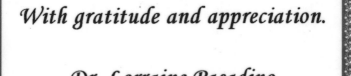

With gratitude and appreciation.

Dr. Lorraine Pasadino
and the CSO Staff

May 20, 1999

Everyday Mysticism

Cherishing the Holy

Wishing you God's Blessings!
Fr. Anthony Ciorra
5/1/99

Anthony J. Ciorra

CROSSROAD • NEW YORK

1995

The Crossroad Publishing Company
370 Lexington Avenue, New York, NY 10017

Copyright © 1995 by Anthony J. Ciorra

Printed in the United States of America

ISBN: 0-8245-1483-1
Library of Congress Catalog Card No.: 95-6659

With respect and love, I dedicate this book
to my parents, Madeline and Louis,
who crossed the ocean to America
to create a more meaningful life
for Pauline, Tina, and me.
They taught us wisdom by showing us
how to find God in the midst of the ordinary.

In appreciation to my sisters and their husbands,
Tina and Tony, Pauline and Lou, and their children,
who have enriched me in so many ways.
Loving them has helped me to be
sensitive to the holy in everyday life.

Contents

Acknowledgments

This book is filled with personal examples of people who have touched my life over the years. The substance of this book is accurate. Names, places, and details have been altered in order to protect people's anonymity. I am grateful for the men and women who so deeply impacted my life in the experiences retold in this book.

This book could not have happened without the support and affection that I have received from so many friends. It is impossible to list all of their names. You know who you are. You have my sincerest thanks. Your friendship means everything to me. Without you, I could never have completed this task.

I would like to acknowledge my colleagues at the College of St. Elizabeth, Morristown, New Jersey, who have been a tremendous blessing in my life. I also owe a great deal to the Sisters of Charity of St. Elizabeth, who have touched my life deeply over the years. They have been a cherished grace for me and my family in so many ways.

I would especially like to thank Dr. Laura Winters and Sr. Alice Lubin, who read my manuscript and offered many invaluable suggestions. Thank you to Fr. Albert Cylwicki and Linda Baratte for so kindly proofreading my manuscript.

I am also grateful to the community of St. Raphael's Parish, Livingston, New Jersey, whose faith and love have sustained and inspired me while writing this book. I am indebted to the priests of Oratory, Summit, New Jersey, with whom I live. They have provided an atmosphere of kindness and generosity in which I was able to spend a lot of time in solitude and study preparing this work. A warm thank you to the Capuchin Friars of St. Mary's Province for their fraternal support.

Thank you also to my friends, Brother Robert Clark, F.M.S., and Dr. Richard Kestenbaum, who also read my manuscript and offered insightful advice.

I would like especially to thank the staff at Crossroad for their graciousness. It has been a pleasure to work with them. Mike Leach, my editor, has been wonderful in offering his wise guidance and enthusiastic encouragement. I am also indebted to John Eagleson for his excellent suggestions and careful reading of the text.

Finally, I want to express my gratitude to Paula Ripple, Fr. Frank McNulty, and Fr. Joseph Champlin for their endorsement of my work, and for their sharing the tremendous wealth of their experiences and talents with me.

Introduction

Nothing here below is profane for those who know how to see. On the contrary, everything is sacred.

— Teilhard de Chardin

Focus Questions

- What is holiness?

- Think of a canonized saint and then think of a living saint.

- What does it mean to be holy today? Think of someone you know whom you consider to be holy.

This is how it all happened. I was leaving the financial district in New York City on a breezy summer evening. I was in a reflective mood. I hurried through the World Trade Center to catch the *Path* train to Hoboken, New Jersey. Since survival is the goal during rush hour, I quickly moved from a reflective mood to a practical mode.

As I joined the crowd and began descending the escalator, I heard the announcement that the train was about to leave. I quickly ran down the steps and made it on the train just in time. Breathless, I stumbled to a seat across from two gentlemen in their early sixties. Call it luck, fate, divine providence, whatever you're comfortable with, but sitting in that particular seat changed my life.

"I find myself longing for some inner peace these days," I overheard one gentleman say to the other. They were both Wall

Street executives on the verge of retirement. It just so happened that they were college classmates who were reminiscing about the "good old days." At one point they both were trying to piece together a poem about solitude that they had learned from their sophomore year English professor. They finally had some idea of what the teacher was trying to communicate about the meaning of life.

"As I look back over my life, at times I'm happy with what I've done, but often I don't feel so good about it all." His friend nodded in agreement. Each seemed to understand what the other meant without fleshing out the details. Their experiences were similar. They both agreed that they weren't satisfied with the quality of life that they lived in the work world. They regretted not spending enough time with their spouses, children, and friends. They also wished that they had developed hobbies and other interests. They gave their lives to Wall Street. They both agreed that if they had to do it over again they would spend their time a little differently.

When the train arrived in Hoboken, we all got off and continued to race to our next destination. As I watched the two businessmen get on their train, I silently said, "Good-bye." I couldn't get them off my mind as I continued on my train. I thought to myself, "Their story would have had a happier ending if they had spent their lives not only achieving financial success but also striving for personal development and interpersonal relationships."

I thought it was a shame that people are so hungry for holiness, and often they do not have the tools for living a spiritually fulfilling life in the midst of the marketplace. The two men changed my life because they started me thinking about what spirituality really means. As I began to reflect on my experience on my way home that night, I recalled that frequently people told me that what they learned about prayer and living a Christian life was no longer working for them in the real world. I also recalled that teaching prayer in seminaries and novitiates was quite different from teaching the same themes in parishes and lay spirituality centers.

On that train ride home that night, I asked myself "Why?" Suddenly it became very clear to me. All that we ever learned about spirituality came out of monasteries and convents. Even diocesan priests had trouble integrating this kind of spirituality into their lives. In a sense, the laity were second-class citizens. They were called to live in the midst of the marketplace. They were taught that real holiness was to be found only in churches and religious communities.

The Vatican Council changed all of this in the 1960s.[1] The council taught that everyone was called to holiness. Its declaration would chart a new voyage for Christian spirituality:

> All in the Church are called to holiness.... It is quite clear that all Christians in any state or walk of life are called to the fullness of Christian life and to the perfection of love. The forms and tasks of life are many but holiness is one.[2]

What is noteworthy is that the Council Fathers had begun to write this chapter about religious life. In mid-course, they switched gears and proclaimed that everyone is called to holiness and that spirituality could be expressed differently according to one's state in life.

As a result of this shift in thinking, Christian spirituality is taking a new turn. Questions such as "What is holiness?" "Is the world a good or evil place?" and "How can we pray in the midst of the marketplace?" are being revisited. On the eve of the third millennium, we are on the cutting edge of what it means to live in relationship to God, the world, and the church. Building on the Christian tradition, twentieth-century spirituality promises to lead us to new places. As we prepare to turn the calendar page to a new century, we must be prepared to begin a new chapter in the history of spirituality.

In its Dogmatic Constitution on the Church, Vatican II made another watershed statement: "The Church...at once holy and always in need of purification, follows constantly the path of penance and renewal."[3] Prior to the council, many viewed the church as a perfect society. From such an opinion about the church it logically followed that perfection would be the goal of the spiritual life. If we admit that the church is imperfect and always in need of reform, it stands to reason that the spiritual journey is now one in which God is discovered in the midst of imperfection.

The findings of contemporary psychology concerning the unconscious negate the possibility of a perfect human being. Because we live in an imperfect world, there is no such thing as perfection this side of heaven. Instead we are in the process of being perfected by God's grace. According to this view, the spiritual life is not a moral state; it is instead a situation of constant growth and development. St. Paul said it this way: "It is not that I have reached it yet, or have already finished my course; but I am racing to grasp the prize if possible, since I have been grasped by Christ Jesus" (Phil. 3:12). The Cappadocian Fathers, Basil, Gregory of Nyssa, and Gregory of Nazianzus developed a spirituality of imperfection by teaching that human weakness is the place where God's initiative creates the process of integration.[4]

As the Fathers of the Second Vatican Council continued their reflections, their final declaration was on "The Church in the Modern World." In this document, written in 1965, the council clearly inserted the church and the Christian in the world. The marketplace and its concerns would be the arena in which Christians would live life and find sanctity. Given this turnaround, people were encouraged to embrace the world rather than to flee from it. This would change the way the relationship between God, prayer, and social action is perceived.

The church took a quantum leap in its universal call to holiness, its admission of imperfection, and its option for the concerns of the world. The two men on the subway reminded me of all of this and spurred me on to write this book. Given the direction of the council, I have chosen to call this work *Everyday Mysticism*. I hope that this book will help resolve the concerns and questions of my subway friends.

Vatican II calls for a new kind of mystic. Thus, in this book I do not use the word "mystic" in the narrower sense of one who experiences visions and ecstasies. I have chosen to use the word mystic in the broader sense of one who is open to meeting God in everyday life. Karl Rahner, whom many consider to be the most important Catholic theologian of the twentieth century, coined the phrase "Everyday Mysticism."[5] His basic teaching was that God could be discovered and experienced in all things. In this sense, everyone is called to be a mystic, finding God in the midst of ordinary human experiences. In this book I use the words "mysticism," "spirituality," and "holiness" interchangeably. All of these words are about finding God in the midst of life.

Everyday Mysticism attempts to redefine holiness from the experience of imperfection to be lived in everyday life. The understanding of holiness has drastically evolved over the centuries. In the Hebrew Scriptures, to be in the presence of the holy was often a shattering and terrifying experience. Gradually holiness became identified with external religious practices. The Hebrews eventually saw themselves as holy, as being set apart. In the Bible, holiness reached its climax in Jesus. With Christ holiness became something that people could touch and see. He used ordinary symbols such as birds, flowers, and mustard seeds to describe the sacred.

The very word "holiness" is the English derivative of the Hebrew word *qds* and the Greek word *hagos,* both meaning "to set apart." It is the notion of setting apart that has been nuanced over the centuries. In this book I propose that the holy is to be found in the midst of the mundane. The sacred is in the ordinary. The holy person looks at the ordinary with wonder and amazement. It is this depth of sensitivity, able to set apart the divine in the midst of the ordinary, that has created our greatest art, music, and literature.

Although we stand on the shoulders of spiritual giants, we are called to a new kind of holiness in the twenty-first century. The blueprint for holiness that helped people from the time of the Council of Trent in the sixteenth century up to the recent past is no longer completely adequate. *Everyday Mysticism* is about the new path and new goals for the spiritual life for the twenty-first century.

Chapter One, "Wisdom on Wall Street," situates spirituality in the marketplace. God is to be found in the context of daily life, often in the unexpected moments and areas of the work place. If the Gospel is to be relevant, it cannot be ignored from nine to five each day during the work week.

Chapter Two, "Dangerous Dreams and Rude Awakenings," places holiness within the life process. Today's theories of personality development poignantly teach that the human person is constantly changing and developing. Our dreams and goals need to be reshaped as we change and as the world and church around us are changing. There are many models in the church's traditional treasury for a spirituality of perfection; there are few for a spirituality of imperfection. Instead of rigid methods, I propose that the process of life offers each person a unique opportunity for holiness.

Chapter Three, "Writing Straight with Crooked Lines," raises some new questions about suffering. Traditional spiritualities that were based on martyrdom and Jansenism often contained a harsh image of God. This chapter challenges some of these notions. God does not cause pain. I suggest a gentle image of God that calls us to growth through our personal suffering as well as through solidarity with the anguish of the world.

Chapter Four, "A Spirituality of Collaboration," challenges the reader to move deeper into human experience. Charity reaches out to those in need. But compassion actually enters into their experience. This leads to a spirituality that finds the sacred in the midst of human feelings. The ultimate discovery is of a prodigal God who is extravagant with the gift of love. Such depth of human and divine association invites all people to collaboration, the highest degree of human interaction and global cooperation.

Chapter Five, "Cunning as Serpents, Gentle as Doves," asserts that the values of the marketplace need to be integrated with the principles of the beatitudes. The marketplace can be transformed through the marriage of these apparent opposites.

Chapter Six, "Mystics in the Marketplace" suggests concrete ways of becoming holy in American culture. It proposes a spirituality based on growing from our imperfections. The principles of Alcoholics Anonymous and the methodology of liberation theology are included in this chapter since their starting points are human weakness and everyday experiences. Ways of praying and reflecting in the world are given to point the reader in new directions for mystical experiences in the marketplace.

Karl Rahner wrote that the future belongs to the mystic. St. Thomas Aquinas said that mysticism is the knowledge of God through experience. A new era in world and church history offers new experiences. A mystic is one who greets the newness with open arms and a welcoming heart. The way to holiness can no longer be universally defined since each person is unique. The ultimate vocation for each of us is to become who we are. That's what it means to be a saint. To become anything else is to do violence to God's creation.

St. Francis of Assisi walked about the world barefooted because he believed that even the ground upon which he walked was holy. Today's holy people will become holy only if their feet are firmly planted on the ground of the marketplace, while their eyes are fixed on the Reign of God that is yet to come. A new millennium calls us to a renewed mysticism that respects the past while creating a new future. Today's mystic is one who cherishes the holy in ordinary daily experiences and can say, "For all that has been — Thanks! To all that shall be — Yes!"[6]

REFLECTION STARTERS

1. Make two columns on a piece of paper. In column one, list the ways you think you are holy. In column two, list the ways that you think you need to change to become holier.

2. What are your imperfections? How can you find God through these?

3. Where's your marketplace? Think about ways you can become holy there.

4. Think of your parents and grandparents. What kind of holiness did they live? How is your way of life and path to holiness different? How do you feel about this?

CHAPTER ONE

Wisdom on Wall Street

All wisdom is plagiarism; only stupidity is original.
— Hugh Kerr

Focus Questions

- Where and when do you feel holy?

- Do you act differently at work than you do at home or at church? Why? Why not?

- What are the ways you can pray in the midst of noise and while doing your daily tasks?

- What is wisdom? Who is the wisest person you know?

- What are the qualities of a good listener?

Monasteries and Marketplaces

Wall Street changed my life.[1] I was a Roman Catholic priest on a sabbatical year working as a businessman at a bank on Wall Street. I was working on my doctoral dissertation and needed to do some experiential work on the relationship between economic systems and theology. Not only did I complete my dissertation and defend it successfully, but also had one of the most interesting and intriguing years of my life.[2] I also learned a lot about life. Rubbing elbows with the Wall Street culture opened my eyes to the tremendous dichotomy that exists between traditional theology and spirituality and the way people live and act in the marketplace.

I'm one of those people who figuratively wore a little black shirt and had a white Roman collar wrapped around my neck from the moment of birth. If anyone wanted to write the Catholic novel about someone who was born in the 1940s, raised in the 1950s, and studied in the seminary in the 1960s, I would be the perfect subject. Catholic from head to toe, I was probably ordained a priest in my mother's womb. Really, could you imagine someone like me working as a bank officer on Wall Street?

Wall Street became a school for me. There I met Sal, one of the holiest persons I've ever known, and George, one of the most corrupt men I've ever encountered. I deeply respected Sal. He was totally unassuming; no task was too undignified for him. He was the epitome of kindness. I just recently found out that Sal has been battling cancer for years. During the year that I was with him, he didn't give the slightest hint that he wasn't well. George was the antithesis of Sal. He was a complainer, a climber, and just a miserable human being. He is the stereotype of the Wall Street executive, ruthless and amoral.

To be honest, maybe there is a touch of Sal and a touch of George in me; maybe all of us have a little bit of each. Like the church, Wall Street is the home of saints and sinners. It's a place where the wheat and weeds grow together. Much to my surprise, I immediately felt at home on Wall Street. I had been heavily involved in administration and priestly formation work in the church. The political and social dynamic of banking was remarkably similar to my ecclesiastical experience. The blatantly obvious overwhelmed me: human nature is basically the same whatever the context.

It dawned on me one day that the church was around before banking. I did some research and discovered that it was actually the church that initiated the banking system in the Middle Ages. I had forgotten the simple reality that some of the same people who show up for church on Sunday are the ones who hold high places on Wall Street on Monday morning.

I learned that year that many of us live schizoid lives. My experience taught me that the Scriptures we read and the liturgy we pray frequently have only a mild impact from nine to five on Wall Street. For many people the values and behaviors stemming from our economic system seem to have a stronger impact on daily life than do the dictates of the Gospel. I found more Georges on Wall Street than Sals. Although the spectrum of people between the poles of Sal and George is quite vast, I don't think that most people would deny that Wall Street is not exactly the place where God's Reign is most clearly and powerfully proclaimed.

Religious people can help to make Wall Street better. The economics of Wall Street can be baptized. It's up to believers to bring a renewed perspective to this economic empire. Pope John Paul II in his recent encyclicals, especially *Sollicitudo Rei Socialis,* challenges the economic systems of both East and West to be more equitable and inclusive of the rights of the poor and oppressed.[3] His teachings can help humanize Wall Street. Christians have something definite to say about restructuring the marketplace.

In addition, Christians in the marketplace have to ask challenging questions about how to pray, be holy, and act lovingly in their work environment. Can the Gospel have any relevance on Wall Street? Is it possible to be happy and fulfilled in the place where I work, where I spend most of my day, in fact, most of my life? Does the Gospel have anything to tell Christians about how to live within the structure of the marketplace?

It dawned on me one day as I was reading a book on the canonization process in the church that Sal probably will never be canonized. Most of the church's official saints are either priests or religious. We need to expand our list of saints to include people who live holy lives in the midst of the secular world. In many respects, their task is even more challenging than that

of the priest or religious since they frequently do not live in an
environment supportive of Gospel values from nine to five.

It's Never Too Late

It is not too late for any one of us to change. As Oscar Wilde
wrote, "The only difference between the saint and the sinner
is that every saint has a past, and every sinner has a future."[4]
The idea of developing a new spirituality for the marketplace
can be frightening. It means letting go of secure assumptions
and categories. The biggest tragedy of the two men I met on
the subway wasn't that they did not use their time well over the
years, but that they thought it was too late to change. They were
stuck in the rut that they created and refused to get out of it.

Like these two men, any one of us can get so lost in what we
are doing that we forget to live life, and then all of a sudden, it
seems as if it is too late. But it's not too late to learn from the
mistakes of others and my own mistakes. I recently had an interesting and inspiring conversation with my sister, Tina, and her
husband, Tony. In the past few years, Tony has begun the practice of going away on a trip each year with his three sons. The
boys are all grown, well into their twenties and early thirties,
and Tony is in his late fifties. Because of a very busy work schedule in his business, Tony did not have this kind of time when the
boys were growing up. He regretted this in later years and knew
that he would do it differently if he had to do it over again. My
sister told him, "It's never too late." And so he started now. He
and the boys, Joseph, Lewis, and Christopher, have a wonderful
time on these trips and look forward to them each year.

I used to tell my students, "I don't care how many mistakes
you make, but please make new ones. Making the same old mistakes is tragic. Making new ones brings excitement and gusto
to life." One of the mistakes of our culture is a work ethic that
stems from a focus on materialism. We work harder and harder
so we can have more and more. We are used to living this way.
It is hard to break the patterns. Our collective mistake is our inability to let go of our desire for more and become satisfied with

less. The most deeply rooted blind spot in our culture is that we think having more will make us happy. Our energies are focused on getting more and more. I remember once taking my nephew, Lewis, when he was a little boy to visit some friends. They gave him a huge dish of ice cream. As soon as it was put in front of him, he immediately started eating the ice cream. I said to him, "Wait a minute, Lewis, what do you say?" He looked up for a fleeting moment and said, "More!" Too often we race out to work in the morning emotionally crying out, "More" without considering the price we're paying.

We've developed our external structures and institutions, but often our interior lives have been neglected. That's the mistake we need to correct. I hope someday I'm on a subway again with the same two gentlemen to tell them it's still not too late. It's possible to be successful and spiritually fulfilled. If we can adjust to wanting what we have rather than having what we want all the time, the pace of life will change. There will suddenly be time and space for many of the things we've always wanted to do.

Religious and Wise

The joining of external success with interior growth is truly the mark of the wise person. The conversion to wisdom is a long and tedious process. Bernard Lonergan taught that there are three types of conversion. The first is intellectual, a changing of ideas. The second is moral, the changing of behavior. The third and highest form of conversion is religious, which means a falling in love.[5]

The conversion to wisdom is a falling in love, a true change of heart. The wise person is the one who knows how to listen, not with the ears but with the heart. Listening with the heart flows from solitude, prayer, and sensitivity and leads to a fuller awareness of self, others, and God.

In the Hebrew Scriptures, Solomon is a symbol of the human person grappling with the conversion to wisdom. His search for wisdom is the ultimate human quest. Wherever or however we

live, we will be happy to the extent that we are wise. Solomon's
story has a lesson for all of us:

> The Lord appeared to Solomon in a dream one night. God
> said, "Ask something of me and I will give it to you."
> Solomon answered: "You have shown great favor to your
> servant, my father David, because he behaved faithfully to-
> ward you, with justice and an upright heart; and you have
> continued this great favor toward him, even today, seat-
> ing a son on his throne. O Lord, my God, you have made
> me, your servant, king to succeed my father David; but I
> am a mere youth, not knowing at all how to act. I serve
> you in the midst of the people whom you have chosen,
> a people so vast that it cannot be numbered or counted.
> Give your servant, therefore, an understanding heart to
> judge your people and to distinguish right from wrong."
> (1 Kings 3:4–9)

The wisdom that Solomon asks for is not to be understood
in abstract or philosophical terms. What he's praying for is
common sense, practical insight in order to judge and lead the
people fairly. Actually, Israel was at a turning point in its faith
journey. The wisdom literature that developed at this time reflected the switch in thinking that suggested that God could be
encountered through human experience. By this point Israel had
a national history that we call salvation history. The questions
for Israel were "Where is God in everyday life?" and "What
does religion have to do with life?" Israel was wrestling with
the question of whether religion makes any difference in the
real world of daily life.

Israel had already come to know God as Savior and Creator,
the one who was responsible for the universe and ordered its
daily workings. Now Israel's task was to find God in the world.
Wisdom is the ability to perceive God in daily life and to live in
harmony with the world. It means paying attention and learning
from daily experience, the key to inner peace and integrity.

Too often we have separated wisdom from religion. Franny,
in J. D. Salinger's *Franny and Zooey,* notes that he heard the

term "wise person" used only once in four years of college.[6]
The religious person can be perceived as the one who obeys the
externals of religious belief, discipline, and worship. Sometimes
such persons might also be wise, but too often they are not.
And this is the problem. Religion that is left in church after a
worship service separates religion from life, thus negating the
experience from which wisdom develops. The task is to bring
religion out on the streets and then to bring the experience of
the streets back into the church. The wise person is the one who
is able to penetrate reality as it truly is and respond accordingly.

Refocus Your Lenses

The Hebrew notion of wisdom taught the people to embrace
the world as it is. This understanding of wisdom culminates
and is completed in Jesus Christ. He is, indeed, the source of
all wisdom who invites us to come and learn from him:

> Come to me, all you who labor and are burdened, and I
> will give you rest. Take my yoke upon you and learn from
> me, for I am meek and humble of heart; and you will find
> rest for yourselves. For my yoke is easy, and my burden is
> light. (Matt. 11:28–30)

Christ offers us an awareness, a way of seeing life. The truly
wise person sees life through Christ's eyes. His is the way of
gentleness and peace.

When I was ordained a priest in 1973, I used to visit St. Anne
Villa, the nursing home for the elderly and retired Sisters of
Charity of Convent Station, New Jersey. I learned a lot about
wisdom from these sisters. Sr. Cecilia Eileen especially touched
me. A victim of multiple sclerosis, she spent most of her religious life, from the time that she was a young sister until her
death in 1976, lying in a hospital bed in the Villa. There was
something very special about her. She always seemed so peaceful and joyful. Whenever I was discouraged, she would tell me,
"Refocus your lenses. Look to the Lord and listen." This was
good advice. In effect, she was actually putting me in touch

with the source of all wisdom. Looking to Christ is the beginning of wisdom. Following, acting, and living like Christ is the demeanor and behavior of the wise person.

Tiny Whispering Sounds

If we were to summarize in one sentence how Christ became a wise person, it might read like this: "Christ is the one who listened to the Father." Christ modeled wisdom by his attentive listening. This kind of paying attention is hard for people living in a fast-paced culture filled with noise and the confusion of so many conflicting voices. Centuries ago, Elijah faced this same challenge:

> Then the Lord said, "Go outside and stand on the mountain before the Lord; the Lord will be passing by." A strong and heavy wind was rending the mountains and crushing rocks before the Lord but the Lord was not in the wind. After the wind there was an earthquake, but the Lord was not in the earthquake. After the earthquake, there was fire, but the Lord was not in the fire. After the fire there was a tiny whispering sound. When he heard this, Elijah hid his face in his cloak and went and stood at the entrance of the cave. (1 Kings 19:11–13)

If we are to become wise, we need to listen to the tiny whispering sounds. Insight is in those tiny sounds. We need to be quiet enough to hear. There are three voices that the wise person has become comfortable with: the voices of self, others, and God. The failure to listen and respond to these voices is to sacrifice personal integration.[7]

It can be said of listening what is often said of charity: it must begin at home. If we have not first learned to listen to our inner voices, it is naive to think even for a second that we can hear God's voice. St. Ignatius of Loyola learned that listening is the way to holiness. He paid attention to the voices that were active within him. His acclaimed method for discerning the spirits came from this simple listening to self. He noticed the differences between those things that brought him short-lived gratification and those that brought him a long-lasting happiness and inner peace.[8]

Make no mistake about it: Ignatius acquired this kind of self-knowledge through a lot of pain and hard work. It required sharp honesty to face himself as he truly was. Taking the mask off, being oneself before God, is the beginning of wisdom. In attempting to communicate this wisdom to us, St. Ignatius suggests an examination of consciousness. This way is far superior and more biblically rooted than our traditional examination of conscience. Rather than taking the minimalistic approach of examining the things that we have or have not done, the greater challenge is to constantly examine our consciousness. What's going on inside of us? What are our needs, fears, angers, hurts, and loves? Because we don't ask these questions, we often miss the deeper realities of life. For unreflective persons, life goes by too quickly, slipping through their fingers.

St. Ignatius's insight into the inner workings of the human spirit is sound psychology. Today psychologists say similar things in a different way. For example, Carl Jung wrote about the importance of balancing the masculine and feminine voices within us, especially as these surface in unconscious drives and symbols. Ira Progoff's intensive journal gives a method for listening to the inner stirrings and concretizing them on paper. Carl Rogers developed an entire system of psychotherapy based on the intensive listening process and unconditional positive regard for the inner feelings of other human beings. Both religion and psychology teach that intensive listening to self is the way to self knowledge, which is the beginning of wisdom.[9]

It all seems so simple. I would like to give an example of how this seemingly easy task is not mastered at times even by the best of us. I have two friends, Michael and Joseph, who are brothers. I love them both. They are real characters. But I have one complaint about them. They don't know how to listen. I remember once watching them from my office window. Michael and Joseph, who are not only brothers but best friends, were out for a walk. They were both talking at the same time, neither listening to the other. In a sense, these two brothers symbolize how many of us walk through life. Great people, but often missing the point of it all because we don't know how to listen.

The Desert in Everyday Life

The key to becoming a listener is knowing how to deal with solitude. Only when we are able to go into our inner desert and acquire the ability of creating quiet moments will we be able to listen to self. The journey inward is the most challenging. We are afraid of that place, so we run from it. But it's only in solitude that we will be able to walk peacefully and joyfully with ourselves, our God, and others.

Slowing down, taking time to hear ourselves is really the Rosetta Stone for discovering God in our lives. God is in the feelings, thoughts, distractions, and dreams of our lives. Listen to your loneliness, listen to your pain, listen to your sexual urges. God is there. God is saying something to you. These tiny whispering sounds within you are the ways in which God is desperately trying to communicate. Divine invitations are constantly being issued to you through the Spirit if only you would listen.

The challenge is to make the desert happen in the midst of the marketplace. It means learning how to take one-minute vacations. Develop eyes and a heart that will notice the beauty in the world even when you are occupied with daily tasks.

I felt this challenge one morning as I was rushing through the World Trade Center. A woman was racing alongside of me, flossing her teeth. I couldn't believe my eyes. She actually tripped over a woman with two children sitting along the outside steps begging for money. I felt for the woman, running and flossing her teeth, because she didn't even notice the poor mother and her children. I stood outside the World Trade Center for two minutes and asked God for the grace to see and feel even as I run. I felt close to God and the woman flossing her teeth and the mother and her two children. Noticing them gave me a lot of food for thought.

God is just as present in the morning rush hour as in the monastery garden or convent chapel. Lunch hours and coffee breaks can be holy moments. Closing your eyes for a few minutes, talking honestly with the people you meet, each can be powerful listening opportunities in the midst of the ordinary and seemingly unholy moments of our day.

The Chinese have an interesting myth about a person lost in the woods. What saves the person is the footprints of an ox that show the way out of the woods. They tell this story to symbolize the plight of every human being. Everyone is lost in the woods. Frequently, people find themselves chasing their tails, caught up in the web of the details of daily life. Call it grace, call it whatever you like, but something calls us to stop and listen to God's voice, not by running away but by staying right where we are. There we find the footprints. This process is called prayer. There's a big difference between saying prayers and praying. The Pelagian perspective places the emphasis on what we must do.[10] However, we are not the ones who begin the process of "lifting our minds and hearts to God." God initiates; we respond. St. Teresa of Avila appreciated this nuance when she taught that prayer is the placing of the mind in the heart, where we listen attentively to the divine stirrings within us.[11]

Listening as a Way of Loving

Either we know how to listen or we don't. If we can listen to ourselves and God, then we can listen to others. Listening is an art that permeates all of life. Just as love is not love until we give it away, listening is not listening until we give it to others. Listening is one of the most wonderful gifts we can offer to others. Jesus tells us that whatever we do for one of these the least his brothers and sisters, we do it unto him (Matt. 25). Listening to people is to love one another. In offering this gift to another, we are offering it to Christ. We cannot claim to be listening to God unless we know how to listen to other human beings. To put it another way: we cannot claim to know how to pray to God unless we know how to listen to human beings.

The Jesus in us is yearning to listen to the Jesus in those around us. Learn to listen to Christ's nonverbal communication in people whom you meet along the way. Christ is speaking through their hurt, anger, loneliness, and the many needs that they express in various ways. Christ is suffering and rejoicing in those around us. Listen to the tiny whispering sounds. They are being spoken constantly, often painfully. Listen. Christ says, "Listen to one another as I have listened to you."

Relationships evolve around speaking and listening to one another. For example, St. Paul had to go to Ananias after his conversion for the laying on of hands (Acts 9). His conversion was incomplete without this interaction with another human being. He had met Christ on the road, but he had not yet met him in his brothers and sisters. Ananias was there to listen to the story and to offer him Christ's gentle touch.

We also have to learn to listen to the unspoken words. St. Francis of Assisi presents a beautiful example of this kind of listening. One day he sensed that one of the friars was having trouble keeping the fast. In response to that need, St. Francis broke the fast with the friar. To make sure he didn't feel guilty, St. Francis invited the whole community to break the fast and have a party. Given the rigid mentality of the church in its fasting regulations in the Middle Ages, St. Francis's action was truly amazing. His sensitivity enabled him to place the needs of his brother before the rules of fasting.[12] This tender quality is the key to good listening. If we cannot listen to one another and minister to one another with sensitivity, then we are working without love.

Having Religion or Being Religious?

When we start to listen with the heart, we will begin to reevaluate the meaning of religion and its meaning in everyday life. We live in one of the most religious periods in the history of Western civilization. One of the dictionary definitions of "religious" is "scrupulously and conscientiously faithful; one who is fervent and zealous." Many people today are faithful to humanity, to the search for meaning and the quest for ultimate values. Although they do not necessarily score high in their adherence to institutional religion and moral values, they are looking for something more from life. In his *Confessions* St. Augustine wrote, "To praise you is the desire of man [sic], a little piece of your creation. You stir man to take pleasure in praising you, because you have made us for yourself, and our heart is restless until it rests in you."[13] The restlessness of the contemporary world is the quest, search, and hunger for God. People may not identify it in this way because they are unaware of their deepest longings. Nevertheless, the yearnings of people today are for that something more, whatever you might call it, to which they can be faithful, zealous, and passionate. Often traditional religious institutions are disappointing to today's generation. These young people challenge organized religions to find new ways of being religious.

In a period when religious, economic, and social institutions are either crumbling or changing, there is much anxiety in the air. When the ancient Chinese wished to place a curse on someone they said, "May you live in a time of transition." I believe transitional times were looked upon negatively precisely because they are filled with uncertainty, worry, and tension. Interestingly enough, the Greek word "crisis" has a double connotation. Negatively, in times of transition everything seems to be falling apart. Things look messy. Positively, crisis can lead to opportunity and growth. I believe that the crisis period in which we now live can be a time of tremendous opportunity for reshaping religious and social paradigms.

We live on the eve of a new millennium. Traditionally, as an era is about to end, people become both nostalgic and apocalyptic. Nostalgia leads them to believe that the yesterdays were better than the todays. Apocalypticism leads them to believe that maybe there won't be a tomorrow.[14] Both of these extremes miss the dynamism and mystery of the present moment. It is in the tension that life is found. To attempt to escape from tension is to escape from life, and to escape from life is to live without enthusiasm. The very word "enthusiasm" means "God is with us." Enthusiasm comes from staying with life's tensions. This is the sign that one's spirituality is real and meaningful.

Traditionally it has been taught that the human person consists of body and spirit. This notion is based on the Greek concept that compartmentalized the human person into these two segments. What was originally intended to assist in understanding the total makeup of the human person became misconstrued in a system that taught that there are really two separate parts to the human person. Among the unfortunate consequences of this compartmentalization is that the spirit was considered to be more important than the body. The body and the material world were understood pejoratively. Thus, to flee from the world and its concerns was the holier and more "spiritual" thing to do.

The World: Good or Bad?

When I was in the novitiate, the mail carrier arrived one day. One of the novices answered the doorbell and started a conversation with him. "When I was in the world," the novice said, "I used to be a mailman." Somewhat bewildered, the mail carrier responded, "When you were in the world! Where do you think you are now?"

I had a similar experience just a few months ago while teaching a course on Christian spirituality. When we completed the section on monasticism, I suggested to the class that we visit a monastery. The day we went to the monastery a carload of monks were driving out as we were entering the front gate. The students said, "Where are they going? We thought that you told us that monks only worked and prayed in the monastery." I responded by explaining to them the need to adapt to situations in the modern world.

When we got into the monastery, one of the monks gave a presentation about monastic life to the students. In passing, he mentioned that women were not allowed in certain sections of the monastery. Asked why, he said, "Because we are fleeing the world!" One of the girls retorted, "You could have fooled me. It seems that these monks that we saw driving out were fleeing the monastery. Besides, when they are driving along in their cars, they're going to see a lot of women out there. That's for sure!"

The monk's remarks to the students epitomized a spirituality that stressed that the world is evil and that we must always prefer the world of the spirit over the domain of matter. The spirituality that I am proposing is the exact opposite. Although there are admittedly different aspects of the human personality, the human spirit and body are both parts of one single entity. To dissect this unity is not only to create a false dichotomy but also to encourage a distorted worldview. The union of body and spirit, heaven and earth, matter and spirit forces us to enter into the reality of the present moment with all of its joys and sorrows, peacefulness and tensions. This spirituality proposes that it is precisely in the stuff that we call real life that God is to be found. The potential for a deep and authentic holiness lies in this messiness where there are more questions than answers.

Karl Rahner believed that the era in which we live is one of the most profound in the history of Western civilization. According to Rahner, Christianity is about to enter a phase in which it will break out of its Hellenistic, institutional mode and become a remnant community. We will be smaller, but stronger and more committed. It will be a recapturing of the spirit that permeated the early churches.

He also predicted the convergence of world religions. No one group can claim to have a monopoly on the truth. Discovering the transcendent means we must dialogue with women and men of different religions, races, and creeds. This calls for a new kind of spirituality, one that embraces the whole world.

Monks must become wise people in their monasteries. The rest of us have to become wise on the world's streets. The agenda of integrating body and spirit and the goal of communion with God and the universe are the same for both monks and people living in the world. But the pathways are quite different. Marketplace spirituality is more challenging because it is relatively new.

To use myself as an example, I was trained in a system that had all the answers. It was painful to suddenly find myself in recent years with more questions than answers. In the disillusionment of this period, I felt myself being challenged to become comfortable with the questions and to find a God who did not dwell in the certainties but in the ambiguities of life. Finding myself at wit's end sparked the real beginning of my spiritual journey. New wisdom comes from letting go of some of the old certainties and living with the questions. That's what it means to be religious and wise on Wall Street.

Conclusion

The Vatican Council called us to a new holiness, a new way of being religious. In this chapter we have seen that wisdom is the bridge that brings us to true religion. In the Judeo-Christian tradition, wisdom occurs in the secular milieu, in everyday life. It comes from paying attention to what goes on around us. This kind of listening to life is what develops and integrates the human person and unites us with the stirrings of the transcendent in the cosmos. Shakespeare's Hamlet was aware of this sensitivity, which is tantamount to holiness: "Give every person thine ear, but few thy voice."[15] The challenge is to live in the world and to be converted to the kind of love that listens attentively to all reality. This kind of holiness can happen anywhere, from monastery gardens to Wall Street banks.

REFLECTION STARTERS

1. Spend a day being conscious of the relationship between the Gospel vision and how you live in the marketplace. Are you an instrument that reflects Jesus' message to the people around you? Do people experience you as being religious in the best sense of that word? Do you feel a need

to change the way you live your life? What changes do you need to make?

2. Rethink an area in your life where you've thought it was too late to change. What can you do to make things a little different?

3. Think back over the last twenty-four hours. What were some of the experiences you had? Do you see God or the call to growth in any of them? Did you listen carefully to the persons and events that came into your life? Did you live wisely? What can you do differently tomorrow?

4. "Conversion": What images does that word bring to mind? Name the ways that you can experience an intellectual, moral, and religious conversion.

5. Spend some time meditating on your death. Picture yourself dying and meeting the Lord. What do you have to tell him about your life? From that vantage point, are you happy about the way you are spending your time each day? If you were to die today, would you be ready and would you be satisfied with the way you had lived?

6. Think about ways it might be possible to get ahead in the marketplace (e.g., economically, socially, or politically) and at the same time remain true to Christian values. Ask the opinion of others.

CHAPTER TWO

Dangerous Dreams and Rude Awakenings

When our first parents were driven out of paradise, Adam is believed to have remarked to Eve: "My dear, we live in an age of transition."

— W. R. INGE

FOCUS QUESTIONS

- Where are you right now in your spiritual journey?

- What are some of the ways that you are different today from the way you were last year at this time? five years ago? ten years ago?

- Can you find God in change, tension, and transition?

Repackaging Holiness

Christian spirituality has been on a straight and narrow path at least since the sixteenth century. The mystical giants of the last four centuries — to mention a few: Ignatius of Loyola, Teresa of Avila, John of the Cross, Francis de Sales, Thérèse of Lisieux —

focused heavily on inner detachment, outward austerity, and a contemplative stance both in the monastery and in the apostolic life. Countless men and women have tried to adapt these spiritualities to their lives in the secular marketplace. Today we need to build on the tradition of monastic spirituality and make new beginnings in developing a secular spirituality for a new kind of mystic.

Holiness in everyday life is not a neat package. To be holy is to change, and to be a saint is to change often. The old spirituality manuals taught that moderation and stability are virtues. The Latin phrase *In medio stat virtus* (virtue stands in the middle) was often cited to support this position. The underlying meaning of the phrase was that extremes were to be avoided and balance is the goal of the spiritual journey. Some people misinterpreted this axiom to mean that any kind of wavering or movement away from the center was not good. Taken to its extreme, this viewpoint implied that change was an imperfection and was often a consequence of original sin. Conformity of dress, speech, and prayer logically followed.

This is no longer an adequate or acceptable way for living in today's world. Contemporary theology, spirituality, and psychology teach about the importance of process and development in life's various stages. Sometimes it might be helpful to move away from the center and stand on the edge. God is also to be found in the risk taking, the struggles, and the passions of daily life. In the changing world and church, it is important that at least some people move from the center and live and speak from the edge.

God's wisdom does not reveal the details of our futures when we say "Yes" to the divine call. God's usual way is to be invitational, without presenting a clearly marked itinerary. Dag Hammarskjold shared this sentiment when he wrote:

> I don't know who — or what — put the question, I don't know when it was put. I don't even remember answering. But at some moment I did answer Yes to Someone — or Something — and from that hour I was certain that

existence is meaningful and that, therefore, my life, in self-surrender, had a goal.[1]

Before I was ordained on May 26, 1973, had I known all that lay ahead, I do not know if I would have had the courage to say "Yes." My response at the time was enthusiastic and sincere. I wanted to give God a blank check, for I shared St. Ignatius's sentiment: "Take, Lord, receive my entire liberty!"

My guess is that this is true for most of us. When you were married, took religious vows, decided to be single, chose a particular career, you didn't know all that was in store for you. You made an act of faith. Have you ever had days when you said, "I wish I knew then what I know now"? I have. For this reason, our act of faith needs to be renewed daily as we face the challenges of each day. The "I do" of marriage vows, the "Poverty, Chastity, and Obedience" of religious vows, and the "I am ready and willing" of priestly ordination are not merely liturgical formulas. These words of commitment must be creatively energized every day in the marketplace.

When I was in college, the big movie hit was *The Sound of Music*. I saw the movie seven times. Last week I saw the movie on the shelf in a video store. When no one was looking, I took it down as if it were X-rated. Certainly, I thought to myself, "*The Sound of Music* is too old fashioned and too schmaltzy for someone like me." Twenty years later I wound up watching it for the eighth time and thoroughly enjoyed it with tears streaming down my cheeks. Maria von Trapp is an outstanding model for not knowing what the future holds and saying "Yes" to uncertainties. Leaving the convent, marrying Baron von Trapp, raising a family, and escaping from Austria to come to America, she was indeed a courageous woman.

The Journey and the Dream

The journey and the dream is an ancient metaphor for human experience. It is rooted in the Hebrew Scriptures. Genesis 12 is the story of Abraham's call and migration. Genesis 12–25 retells the story of Abraham and Sarah's faith struggles. Their response to God often paled in the face of trials and tribulations.

Abraham and Sarah symbolize the sincerity and the fickleness of our human "Yeses." They were willing to go on the dangerous journey to which God invited them and dream the dream of being parents even in their old age. They often stumbled along the way. They doubted. They sinned. They were ready to renege on their covenant with God. Ultimately, they proved their fidelity in their willingness to sacrifice their son Isaac. But they didn't achieve this all at once. Theirs was a faith that survived many failures. They had to make many serious adaptations in how they lived and responded to God's invitations. All that finally mattered was their willingness to sacrifice their son. They had learned the lesson and thus became our "Father and Mother of Faith," models for pilgrims on the spiritual journey.

The Eastern church has a marvelous image of God: God is the Divine Dancer. This image is a dynamic one in which humans are invited to be re-created through a relationship with God. As compared to the static Creator image, it emphasizes the constant renewal of the human person, learning to dance according to God's rhythm, allowing God to lead. This is challenging. We can resonate with Frank Sinatra when he sings, "I'll do it my way." Wisdom is really learning to let go of our hard-headed self-willfulness and learning to do it God's way.

Israel's watershed was its experience of being saved in the Exodus. It was the Exodus that fashioned Israel into a people. This experience of God as savior, who freed the people from the slavery of the Egyptians, is the event that encouraged Israel to trust Yahweh and to dance according to God's rhythm, wherever that might lead.

The Exodus experience is the protomyth of the Jewish people. Myth does not mean falsehood. It means an event or experience so powerful that it forms people into a cohesive community. The Exodus and the crossing of the desert were such events for the Jewish people. These events are paradigmatic for all who embrace the Judeo-Christian tradition. Even though we may waver in our commitments, the Exodus paradigm assures us that God is forever faithful and never ceases to offer us freedom and life. In the faith journey we discover that God is savior, the one who leads, who will not abandon us. God is the beginning, the middle, and the end of the journey.

Eight hundred years ago, St. Bonaventure wrote in *The Journey of the Soul into God* that every vocation is a journey. He approaches the journey theme from the inner experience of the human person, suggesting that the pilgrim on life's journey passes through certain phases of growth. The first is the movement outside oneself looking for meaning in the world. In this first phase, the world of nature and the physical universe are the places to find meaning. This accomplished, the pilgrim is next ready for the more dangerous journey within the self. The traveler will go to inner levels never thought possible. This self-discovery will bring a new awareness of our innermost feelings and most hidden thoughts. The final stage of the journey is the most courageous of all, the movement beyond oneself to the transcendent God. Once we surrender on this level, we have no idea where we'll be going. We allow God to be in control of our life.[2]

An image illustrating St. Bonaventure's ultimate phase of the journey is Jesus Christ disguised as a hitchhiker. As the driver notices the person on the road, there are several options. The first is to keep on driving and to ignore the hitchhiker. The second is to invite the person into the car. The third option is to stop the car, get out of the driver's seat, and allow the hitchhiker to get in and drive. This is what St. Bonaventure means by allowing God to the center of your life. That's the ultimate purpose of the constant reshaping of our dreams. Until that decision is made to let go of control and allow God to be in the center, the traveler will be unsettled.

Life's Stages and the Spiritual Journey

The journey toward God is a lifetime affair. Developmental psychologists describe human beings as going through stages. From a religious point of view, each stage has the potential of deepening our understanding of God and bringing God closer to the center of our lives.[3]

The story of Joseph and his brothers is an important paradigm in the Hebrew Scriptures (Gen. 38–45). Certainly Joseph was deeply hurt by the rejection and cruelty of his brothers. His ability to let go of that wound in later years was freeing not only for him but also for his brothers. A critical axiom for growth along life's stages is the necessity of working through the hurts and scars that we acquire along the way.

I did not always love telling the story of how I stayed back in the first grade. Now I tell the story quite freely and always manage to get a few good laughs from my audience. I've come to enjoy the story.

Sr. Noël was fresh out of the novitiate. She could not have been more than twenty years old. Of course, in the traditional religious habit, she seemed ageless. I didn't fare too well in the first year of my educational career. At the end of the year, Sr. Noël called me into the cloak room and said to me, "Anthony, I have a very busy year coming up next year. I have so much work to do, I just don't know how I'm ever going to do it alone. Do you think you could stay on for another year and give me a hand?" If for no other reason, I deserved to stay back because I was thrilled beyond words that Sr. Noël had chosen me from among the whole class "to stay on for another year." Going home that day, I told my classmates what had happened. Suddenly I became a superstar. They were all jealous that they were not staying back. They ran to the convent and rang the doorbell. When Sr. Noël answered, they all pleaded, "Please, Sister, can we stay with Anthony? We want to help you next year. We'll stay on for another year too."

That summer I had to make up for a lot of reading that I missed during the year. Each morning when I woke up, my mother would spend three hours going over the reader with me. My mother was born in Italy. She would read, "Looka Dick, he'sa chasin Spot. Spots a chasin Jane. Jana is a chasin Dick."

By the end of the summer I mastered the first grade reader and developed an Italian accent.

When I returned to school in September, Sr. Noël was transferred. My new first grade teacher was Sr. Catherine Maurice. She called on me the first day of school to read. I stood up as proud as a peacock with reader in hand before the entire class. When I began reading with my Italian accent, everyone started to laugh. I was confused. I didn't know why they were laughing. At the end of the day, Sr. Catherine called me into the cloak room. I thought to myself, "Here we go again!" When Sr. Catherine corrected me on my Italian accent, all I could say was, "Does this mean that I have to stay on for another year?"

Even though I like telling this story, for a number of years I didn't think it was so funny. The memory, in fact, was painful. This became one of my early life hurts that needed healing. For a few years, I was stuck there. I didn't see myself as worthwhile. I felt awkward and resentful that I was a year older than everyone in my class.

A basic principle is that we must deal with the baggage of each developmental stage of life if we are going to advance to the next stage. I share my first grade story to illustrate a powerful memory that stands out in my mind as I reflect on the phases of my journey. I had to deal with this hurt if I was to mature properly. If I were not so fortunate as to have many healing and successful experiences, especially in education, I could have easily become locked into the negative emotional state of a first grader who could not make it with the rest of the class.

A lot has been written in recent years about the stages of maturation. I would like to look briefly at these stages of life's journey and make application to opportunities for faith and spiritual development.

Life beyond the Womb. Even within the womb, the fetus can detect its mother's feelings and the tone of the surrounding environment. The fetus senses acceptance or rejection. The way a child is received into the world and enters into a family leaves an indelible mark on the child's spirit.[4]

Paul is one of my closest friends. He is sixty years old and emotionally immature. When he was in his early twenties, he learned that his mother did not want to be pregnant with him and that she even attempted an abortion. He told me that he intuited a feeling of rejection from the time he was a young boy. He was devastated when his worst fears were confirmed. The rejection in his mother's womb has colored his whole life. At the age of sixty he is still insecure and overly sensitive. Indeed, life's joys and sorrows begin in the womb.

Beyond the womb, the degree to which we will be able to trust and enter into relationships in later years is heavily influenced by the faithfulness and love of our parents in the first few years of life. If mother and father can be counted on to care for our needs, then God and other people can be trusted.

Jean, a woman in her early thirties, came to me for counseling. Her parents had divorced when she was five years old. All she can remember of her father is that he beat her mother and always punished her. Now she has a hard time relating to men. It saddens me that the idea of God as Father or Mother are both repulsive to her. She has consistently entered into relationships that are abusive. It will take a long time of continued therapy before she can be healed.

Our sense of self-worth is greatly influenced by the treatment we are given in the first five years of life. Everyone agrees that these are the most formative and important years. Venturing out of the security of home into the world of school and peer relationships affects our ability in later years to take risks in new ventures. The degree of success and the quality of love and security experienced in this developmental phase will profoundly affect the entirety of our life.

I recall a very moving example of a young boy, Jerry, whom I taught in class when I was first ordained. I was assigned to teach religion to the first, second, and third grades. For the first two years of class, Jerry would not talk to anyone. We never heard his voice. He just looked and acted sad. But the principal and faculty would not give up on him. When Jerry was in the third grade, I was teaching his class a new song. It was an interactive song, where the students responded to a line that was sung to them. I spontaneously addressed the song to Jerry, "Hey, Jerry, do you love Jesus?" And for the first time in three years, we heard his voice as he sang back, "Oh, yes, I love Jesus." I was moved to tears.

As Jerry began to talk, the school psychologist discovered that Jerry's mother was an alcoholic and abused him terribly. This explained his silence. The love and affirmation given to him by our staff was the beginning of his healing process. In later years, Jerry suffered an addiction to drugs. More healing, programs, and love were still needed. Jerry still carries baggage from those early years. I continue to hope and pray that the scars will be healed so he can get on with his life.

When you begin to realize the pain that young children carry with them, Jesus' appreciation of children becomes even more touching and meaningful. He taught us we should deal with children: "Let the children come to me. Do not hinder them. The Reign of God belongs to such as these" (Matt. 19:13–15). The delicacy and sensitive care we should offer to all children is clearly admonished: "Better that a millstone be tied around your neck and you were thrown into the sea than to give scandal to one of these little ones" (Luke 17:2). We must both look to the child within us who needs to be healed and to be deeply aware of how we have the power to bless or destroy the children who come into our lives.

Living with the Monster. Jesus is a wonderful symbol of the struggles to move beyond childhood into adolescence. The Jesus who was lost in the Temple at the age of twelve was a source of confusion to Mary and Joseph. I have often wondered what they must have thought when he responded to their "Where were you?" with "I must be about my Father's business." Jesus at this point in his life demonstrates the tension that exists between parents and children who are moving into that in-between stage of life.

The adolescent can generalize from concrete life experiences to more abstract principles. This allows the adolescent to consider answers to the questions of life, such as the meaning of God, religious principles, and personal values. The period between the ages of twelve and eighteen is a time of religious awakening when people are converted or abandon the faith taught during childhood. Around age thirteen, many begin to question earlier teachings. This is the beginning of another evolution in understanding self, others, and God.

James Fowler writes that interpersonal relationships are the primary concern in early adolescence (ages thirteen to eighteen).[5] The human person begins to question and rely on the views of others to help construct a value system and begin to take ownership of personal beliefs. Erik Erikson suggests that now the adolescent begins to forge an identity.

Adolescents often develop defense mechanisms to avoid this painful process. These escapes may take the form of drugs, alcohol, sexual activity, and excessive TV watching. They also might find gratification in roles, for example, athlete or scholar. This is a time of rebellion. Often the adolescent will take on values that directly offend parents, teachers, and other authority figures. These are outward expressions of the deep confusion of this phase of life.

One author entitled his book on adolescent psychology *Living with the Monster.* Interestingly enough, he meant this both from the adolescent and parental vantage points. Adolescence can be an incredibly painful time in one's life, both for the adolescents and anyone associated with them. The young adult wrestles with God, the church, and all authority symbols.

Teaching religion to sophomore boys was one of the greatest challenges I've ever faced. I never knew what they were going to say or do next. One year I was asked to teach them a course on the Gospel of St. John. On the first day of class, I referred to John 3:23. They chimed in, "Do you mean the bathroom on the third floor?" When I was trying to teach them about God's forgiveness through the Mary Magdalene story, I said,

"She was the town prostitute." They looked pretty bored. To arouse some interest, I said, "Well, what would you think if you saw the town prostitute walking down the street with me?" A boy from the back of the room bellowed, "She would have to be pretty hard up!" There were days with these students when I didn't know whether to laugh or cry. And that's how it is living with adolescents, because they don't know if they want to laugh or cry.

As in the entire spiritual journey, it is important to encourage adolescents to pay attention to their experiences and not to be afraid of them. God is in the experience, even if it be confusion and chaos. We need to tell people that it is okay to be where they are, that they do not have to escape the pain of the darkness.

The uniqueness of every adolescent needs to be affirmed. Their quest for relationships should be reverenced, even though there will be mistakes along the way. They must respect their feelings and be challenged to take healthy risks in their relationships. It is important that sensitive adults be present to young people to help them to reflect on and grow from these events. Young people are faced with great challenges. They must discover themselves, learn how to enter into deeper, loving relationships, move away from parental control, and strive to find a place in the adult world. The historical Jesus, especially as depicted in Mark's Gospel, who had feelings, questions, temptations, and struggles, can be an excellent inspiration and companion for this developmental phase.

Birthing Adulthood. These categories of developmental phases are somewhat artificial, for most people do not experience life in a mathematical progression. But they do help us to appreciate the characteristics of human growth.[6] Given this caveat, some developmentalists think that the transition from later adolescence to young adulthood takes place between the ages of nineteen and twenty-two. This desert period is often a time of even more intense questioning and distressing loneliness. My friend Jeff wrote me a letter during such a time in his life:

Dear Father Tony,

Unfortunately I find I need to dump on you. You see I find myself so burdened lately with so many problems that I'm about to expire or more likely explode. I'm finding it so difficult to juggle so many things all at once. If I told you the things that have happened to me lately, you just wouldn't believe it.

Honestly, I don't know what is keeping me together. Days melt into one another, pain haunts me, and yet somehow I wake up for another mindless day. I'm not exaggerating when I tell you that I have been torn apart by my pains, problems, and friends. I hurt so much at times that if I were to pray to God, he would get nothing but hateful things from me, so I have just about shut him out of my heart. Praying is a comfort that I have lost.

It's taken a lot for me to write this letter. I've wanted to speak with you for so long to share my pains, but all good things elude me lately. Why? Who really knows? I'm so empty that feelings are very hard to raise within me. Hope is my most trusted friend. Somehow, I hold on to hope like the rust on a piece of an old chain. I constantly hope for better days.

I tell you I'm tired, so very tired of being ill that it's making me sick. I find it affecting me more and more lately. It's creeping into my attitude and poisoning me. I find myself always putting up a good front or forcing myself to do things, especially when I don't feel like it.

I'm sorry I dumped all this on you. Believe me, there are tons of good things to tell you. I think.

Love,
Jeff

Jeff's letter is typical of the angst of the early stages of young adulthood. His letter captures the mood of this transitional period. Much of the loneliness and alienation stems from the uncertainties about future directions. Skepticism about institutional values can leave the adolescent in limbo. Unsettlement may mount well into the late twenties in the young adult's life. Twenty-nine is often called the mythical death age. It is the final dying to youth and cementing one's feet firmly into the world of adulthood.

Recall that Israel's path was anything but a straight road. We need to be careful to know when to challenge people to grow and when to accept them where they are. Parents and other authority figures can unwisely pressure young adults to resolve issues and answer questions prematurely. Everyone needs to relax with ambiguity. God is in the painful feelings of uncertainty. Learning this lesson helps us to accept the imperfections of others.

People mature at different rates. People give the appearance of adulthood in their mid-twenties and are expected to act accordingly. But adolescent issues continue to linger for many of us well into our mid- to late twenties. Often young couples struggle with marriages during this time because they were not emotionally ready for this kind of commitment. Others find that their career path is not what they thought it would be and want to make some significant adjustments. It is not too late to make these painful changes. The temptation is to pretend that life is running along smoothly. Honesty with feelings is essential for the changes now needed.

The Thirsting Thirties. Being successful is the goal for most people in their thirties. Productivity in the world is especially important now. Most adults race through their thirties with a multitude of tasks. These years also provide an opportunity to correct the mistakes of the twenties and to make a clear mark on the world.

The thirties are characterized by constant building. David and Solomon's efforts in constructing the temple and Israel's spiritual identity are powerful role models for the thirties. David and Solomon's vision and energy brought about the temple and made Israel into a nation. These two men are to be admired for their zeal for the house of the Lord and the good of God's people. Accepting challenges, working hard, and rolling up one's shirt-sleeves are characteristic of the thirties. Conversely, self-serving and feverish activity can be counter-productive. Prayers of the saints, such as Ignatius of Loyola's prayer for generosity and Francis of Assisi's prayer for peace, can be helpful in keeping energy creatively channeled during the thirties.

People in their thirties need to be careful that they do not use all their energies to achieve success and thereby ignore other aspects of life. My friend Alex's life is all too typical. In his thirties, he made a lot of money, owned two homes, and had a beautiful car. Meanwhile, he paid little attention to his wife, Mary Jane. He always worked late into the night. When he got home, he was exhausted and in no mood for conversation. He became a miserable human being. He was impossible to live with. Mary Jane found someone else who was able to meet her emotional needs and eventually divorced Alex. Their story is a reminder not to forget what's really important in life as you strive for material and financial success.

The Mid-Life Crisis Club. Mid-life is that interesting time that has been called the old age of youth and the youth of old age.[7] Mid-life has become a popular topic for conversation. In fact, having a mid-life crisis has become avant-garde. I even know a group of suburbanites who have formed a mid-life crisis club. Having experienced a mid-life crisis myself, I can say that they are scary but wonderful. Although I found myself saying during this time, "Damn, will it ever let up?" my mid-life crisis was one of the best things that ever happened to me. Just when we think that everything is settled in life, we discover that there are more adjustments to be made. Although this is emotionally and phys-ically exhausting, growth will occur to the degree that we are willing to make the necessary alterations at this point in life. I remember finding myself tired of playing games and assum-ing roles. Because I finally faced questions and issues that I ran from for years, mid-life became a time that I truly blossomed and became comfortable with the person God made me to be.

Somewhere between forty and sixty, the limits of life become strikingly obvious. This is most clearly felt in the body. The tipoff is when you find yourself saying, "It never hurt in this spot before." The body isn't able to do all that it used to do. Signs of aging remind the mid-lifer that death will arrive one day. Many people once again reassess their commitments and accomplishments. To get to the bottom line, the questions at this point are: "What have I done with my life?" and "What do I want to do with the rest of my life?"

From a religious perspective, mid-life is a good time to go on a few retreats, giving yourself the time and space needed to take stock and reorient your life. It's an opportunity to learn a few new skills, like journal techniques and dream analysis, that can facilitate the inner journey. The great lesson to be learned in mid-life is surrender to the process and allowing life to take its course. It is a time for letting go, mourning losses, and celebrating spiritual, emotional, and relational resurrections.

Elderhood. When we talk about old age, we need to remember that these can be the most precious and important years of life.[8] Luke's presentation of Anna symbolizes that possibly the best is yet to come in old age:

> Anna had seen many days, having lived seven years with her husband after her marriage and then as a widow until she was eighty-four. She was constantly in the temple, worshipping day and night in fasting and prayer. Coming on the scene at that moment, she gave thanks to God and talked about the child to all who looked forward to the deliverance of Jerusalem. (Luke 2:36–38)

Anna is a wonderful symbol for our culture, which often denies the sacredness of old age. In her old age, her life's dreams were fulfilled, and she played a significant role in welcoming the savior.

The final years of life, from sixty-five onward, are called elderhood. Since I haven't experienced this phase of life yet (although it's not far off!), I'm using other people's insights, especially my mother's. She recently turned ninety. It is hard to watch her grow old. I see her physically slowing down. There's a lot that she cannot do anymore. Although I feel bad for her, I often sense that in the midst of her physical pain, she has a deep inner peace. She has resolved many of the issues left over from earlier life stages.

Nobody wants to grow old, but, as Mark Twain observed, "It's preferable to other alternatives." Growing old is especially painful in a culture like ours that deifies youth. Old age is a time to mourn losses of friends, family, and bodily vigor. It offers yet another opportunity for the healing and reconciliation of life's hurts. It is a reminder to us that there is no final cure. There comes a point when doctors and other health care professionals have done all that they can do. The ultimate questions of life, death, and what next become increasingly difficult to avoid.

Old age is a time of disengagement from the duties and responsibilities in the work force. Although older people are no longer productive in this way, they have a lot of wisdom to share. We would be foolish not to capitalize on their wealth of experience. The elderly are a valuable and precious asset; we are privileged to have them among us.

Elderhood especially lends itself to contemplation. "Contemplation" is a word that we may have tossed around quite freely in our younger years. But at earlier periods of life we are often too preoccupied and busy for quiet prayer. It's only in old age that we are ready for this kind of quiet union, gazing, wasting time, just being there, with our Beloved. The physical limitations and fewer time commitments of old age offer the opportunity for lengthier prayer time and a peaceful rhythm that lends itself to contemplative moments.

José Barrios is a wonderful example of someone I knew who grew old gracefully. He had successfully worked through the developmental stages. When I first met him, he was eighty years old, and I was twenty-six. I was assigned to his home parish of St. Thomas the Apostle in Bloomfield, New Jersey.

When I arrived, José told me that he wanted to be a deacon and asked if I would be his mentor. Naively thinking that I was eminently qualified for this task, without hesitation I said, "Yes." I didn't realize at the time that José would actually become my mentor. I learned more from him than from any professor or seminary textbook.

At the age of eighty-three, he was ordained a deacon and had more life and energy than many people in their twenties. I used to go on hospital visitation with him. I couldn't keep up with him. After a full day of hospital visits, he would want to go visit the old people in the nursing home, although he was older than most of the "old people."

José died a beautiful death, singing on his way to the operating room, thanking God for the blessings he experienced in life. He left a powerful legacy. He taught us how to grow old elegantly, how to work through life's hurts effectively, and how to make the best contributions to society in old age. By example, he showed us how to live life. He reached life's goal: José was a truly wise man.

When we look at life's stages all at once, it can all seem so overwhelming. Each person is different. It is impossible to program the details of where life is going. However, we can at least get a sense of the broad strokes, the basic rhythms and directions of life. A woman who was 105 years old in a nursing home, as cheerful and alert as could be, gave me great advice when she told me to cheer up: "The first hundred years are the hardest. After that it's a breeze." She shared with me a prayer of Pierre Teilhard de Chardin that she had been saying for the past thirty years:

> Above all, trust in the slow work of God.
> We are, quite naturally,
> impatient in everything to reach the end
> without delay.
> We should like to skip
> the intermediate stages.
> We are impatient of being
> On the way to something unknown,
> something new.

And yet it is the law of all progress
that it is made by passing through
some stages of instability
and that it may take a very long time.

And so I think it is with you.
Your ideas mature gradually,
let them grow,
let them shape themselves,
without undue haste.
Don't try to force them on,
as though you could be today
what time (that is to say,
grace and circumstances
acting on your own good will)
will make you tomorrow.

Only God could say what this new spirit
gradually forming within you will be.
Give our Lord the benefit of believing
that his hand is leading you,
and accept the anxiety of feeling yourself
in suspense and incomplete.[9]

Taking a Vow Is a Dangerous Thing

In the face of all the twists and turns of life, it is impressive
when someone has the courage to say "Yes" to any kind of
a commitment. Recently I was celebrating the wedding liturgy
of a wonderful young couple, whom I deeply admired and respected. The theme of their wedding liturgy was "Taking a Vow
Is a Dangerous Thing." You have to have a lot of love in your
heart to promise forever, because only God knows where it will
all lead.

In his play *The Skin of Our Teeth*, Thornton Wilder beautifully illustrates this point:

MRS. ANTROBUS: (*calmly, almost dreamily*): I didn't marry
you because you were perfect. I didn't even marry you

because I loved you. I married you because you gave me a promise. (*She takes off her ring and looks at it.*) That promise made up for your faults. And the promise I gave you made up for mine. Two imperfect people got married, and it was the promise that made the marriage.[10]

Promises are built on dreams. Many of these dreams are formulated during youth. Most people strive to make these dreams mature during the adult years. The fundamental dream is similar for most Christians. This came home to me recently at a nun's eightieth jubilee celebration. Her provincial prayed a beautiful blessing over her: "May this celebration deepen within your heart your dream of younger years, the dream to be a holy person." As I cut through all of the extraneous details of my life, I know that the words of this prayer are true for me. Even though I didn't articulate it in that way, my desire for priesthood was really a desire for holiness. Because I have often not lived up to that ideal, I'm challenged by the words of the book of Revelation, "Wake up. I find that the sum of your deeds is less than complete in the sight of God. Change and return to your earlier ways" (Rev. 3:2–3).

Dreaming Holy Dreams

I've been trying to become holy for years now, without much success. Even in the seminary, I was determined to become holy. I developed a one-year plan. I would work on a different virtue each month. At the end of the year, I would have mastered the twelve essential virtues of the Christian life. At the end of the first month, I was thrilled because I had mastered humility. I was finally able to say, "Now I am truly humble." I was ecstatic by the twelfth month when I had mastered charity, the greatest gift of all (1 Cor. 13). I felt wonderful. The following September a new student came into our class from another diocese. We disliked each other from the start. What bothered me most wasn't that we didn't get along, but that I just did not want to like him. And a whole year's work in mastering the virtues went right down the tubes.

When I was ordained, I thought I would give it another try. My first assignment was to a large suburban parish of four thousand families, twenty thousand people. These people loved me and were very good to me. At age twenty-six, I was too young to appreciate how blessed I was to be with such wonderful people. They taught me a lot about holiness, just by being who they were, loving, generous, and kind. I wanted to be holy, but I didn't feel holy. This disturbed me. After three years in the parish, I was sent to teach high school boys. I loved it. These were happy, wonderful years. But I still didn't feel holy enough. The dream kept nagging me.

I thought to myself, "Maybe, I should be a monk. That's certainly a way of giving my all to God." I started to visit the Trappist monks at St. Joseph Abbey in Spencer, Massachusetts. Their monastery is one of the most beautiful places I've ever seen. The liturgy is the best I've experienced anywhere. I loved it there. I thought to myself, "Now, this is a place where I could be really holy." When I spoke to the abbot and novice master, they indicated that the monastery might be for me. But something kept nagging me, "I can't be a monk; I like to be with people, and I like to talk. Could I keep quiet most of the day?" I listened to my feelings, and, reluctantly, I decided not to enter.

I continued my conversations with the abbot, and he shared much of his wisdom with me. I confided in him, "I don't feel holy. What do you think I can do about it?" He responded, "Nothing." He advised me not to concentrate on my efforts but rather let God lead the way. "God will make you holy in due time," he said. I responded by saying, "I want to be there now." I gradually came to realize that I really didn't understand what the word "holy" meant. I had associated it with external appearances and actions rather than an attitude toward life. One of the monks quoted George Orwell to me: "Many people genuinely do not wish to be saints, and it is probable that some who achieve or aspire to sainthood have never felt much temptation to be human beings."[11] I was finally at peace. I understood that my holiness rested in my humanness and willingness to continue along on the journey each day.

Holiness in My Own Backyard

We've all had dreams. Thank God for the dreams that we've had. It would be sad to live life without them. My dream to be a monk led me to deeper growth even though I never actually became a professed monk. I adjusted my dream and became a monk in my heart. We need to reshape our dreams at each developmental life transition. The challenge is to make our goals happen. The ultimate lesson to be learned is that the power to fulfill our deepest hopes lies within our own backyard. Happiness is within our hearts, not in the fulfillment of external goals and success. It is simply a matter of perception.

The real is how we actually live our lives. The ideal is something outside ourselves. The task is to mix the pure ideal with the realities of daily life. Physical capabilities, strengths, weaknesses, and native intelligence need to be considered carefully each time we reshape our ideals.

It's hard to balance all of this. A lot of people that I met on Wall Street were working hard to maintain a lifestyle and to fulfill dreams that were implanted deep within their hearts since childhood. Many of these goals have collapsed due to shifting economic and political events. Many benefits that the older generation took for granted, like owning a home and having the best in health care, are no longer possible for younger generations. America isn't what it used to be. People will have to make a lot of changes. What is needed are new dreams of a simpler lifestyle.

Everything changes, even in the church. One author wrote that many priests are either angry about the people who don't come to church or are angry about what those who do come do when they get there. The church of the 1950s is gone. In itself, that's neither good nor bad. It is easy to get angry when the symbols that held us together in the church for so many years are no longer present. Some of the old dreams have been shattered. Now our inner peace, happiness, and effectiveness as a sign of God's Reign depend very much on our willingness to reshape our dreams.

Many theorists have written about these stages.[12] Most writers agree that people usually begin with a deep idealism about life and their future. At some point, usually in early adulthood, they begin to realize that the world, church, and people do not fully measure up to all their expectations. This is the turning point. This realization makes some people bitter for life. Others, tempered by reality, make the necessary adjustments and dream new dreams.

The Second Yes

Saying "Yes" to God and other people early in life and dreaming great dreams are exciting and important phases of our human development. I don't think that the journey really begins, however, until we've had a few rude awakenings, realizing that life, God, the church, the world, and even ourselves aren't all that we thought they would be. Then we're ready to renew life-long commitments.

My friends Jim and Virginia recently renewed their wedding vows on their fiftieth wedding anniversary. Their life has been filled with its share of ups and downs. Sometimes God seemed to throw them a curve ball or two. In the midst of it all, they have always had the ability to see the positive in life. As I have known them over the years, I find them more in love and loving every time I see them.

I couldn't hold back the tears when they said "I do" at their fiftieth. It was deeply moving and powerfully impressive. Jim and Virginia love each other more today than they did fifty years ago. At the reception Jim sang a love song to Virginia. Even though it was off key, it was one of the most beautiful songs I've ever heard because it came from the depths of his heart, filled with fifty years of experience.

The model of the second "Yes" is rooted in the New Testament. After saying "Yes" to the Lord and promising him so much, St. Peter was really a failure as a disciple. Only in the experience of failure did he become a true disciple. St. John tells the story this way:

> When they had eaten their meal, Jesus said to Simon Peter, "Simon, son of John, do you love me more than these?" "Yes, Lord," he said, "you know that I love you." At which Jesus said, "Feed my lambs."
>
> A second time, he put his question, "Simon, son of John, do you love me?" "Yes, Lord," Peter said, "you know that I love you." Jesus replied, "Tend my sheep."
>
> A third time Jesus asked him, "Simon, son of John, do you love me?" Peter was hurt because he had asked a third time, "Do you love me?" So he said to him: "Lord, you know everything. You know well that I love you." Jesus said to him, "Feed my sheep." When Jesus had finished speaking he said to him, "Follow me." (John 21:15–19)

This second call of Peter came after he had dreamed many dreams, gone on a few detours, and experienced some rude awakenings. This second call was certainly the most powerful and profound of all of the events in his life. In our religious, married, single, or priestly lives we need to go through a similar process. After we've reshaped the dream a few times, we will discover that the best is yet to come. Then we are invited to say "Yes" again. There might be a few battle scars, some wounds, and a trembling voice, but that second "Yes" is a mark of the mature disciple.

A Monk in the Marketplace

The past twenty years have been ones of future shock. Since the Second Vatican Council, the church, once so stable an institution, has become fragmented in its beliefs and has lost some of its credibility. The Vietnam War and Watergate triggered a similar disintegration in American society. No one told us to fasten our seat belts because no one really saw all of this coming. Role models for these times are few and far between.

I have a hero, someone who embodies the themes and transitions of our times. Thomas Merton is a strong symbol of a Christian who lived through these transitions and became more mature and holier in the process. The vibrancy in Merton's life came from his constant willingness to respond openly to new circumstances and experiences.

After Thomas Merton wrote his *Seven Storey Mountain* in 1948, sixty books and three hundred published articles followed. Many believe that Merton may turn out to be the most significant Christian figure of the twentieth century. Merton captured the spirit of our age and models for us how to live creatively in these times.

His life was always changing, adapting to the times and circumstances. All his life was a search for meaning. He thought that when he found God, or, as he puts it, "when God found me" and he went into the monastery, his search had ended. In fact, it was just the beginning of endless searching. Merton would have to change again and again if he was to continue to be authentic.

Thomas Merton was born in France in 1915 to an English father and an American mother. He converted to Roman Catholicism in 1938 and became a Trappist monk in 1941. His autobiography, *The Seven Storey Mountain,* was a best-seller in 1948. It was the story of his conversion. Merton was truly a contemplative who was able to combine within his monastic life a keen concern for the social issues of our day. In his later years he became interested in Eastern religious experience. He died following this concern while in Bangkok. Ironically, in 1968 his body was flown home on a plane with bodies of soldiers killed in the Vietnam War, of which he passionately disapproved.

I discovered Thomas Merton in the late 1970s while I was doing graduate work at St. Bonaventure University. Merton had taught there from 1938 to 1941. St. Bonaventure's was a special place for him and for me. He discovered his Trappist vocation there while praying before a statue of St. Thérèse of Lisieux. He loved hiking the great Allegheny mountains. He had some special friends there, like Fr. Irenaeus, the librarian. During my time at St. Bonaventure's, many of these places and people also became special for me. It was through them that I got in touch with the spirit of Thomas Merton.

He wrote sections of his *Seven Storey Mountain* at the university, and the original manuscript is in the library. I became friendly with Merton's friend, Fr. Irenaeus, who was still the librarian. I talked him into letting me have the manuscript for a couple of hours. He made me promise not to photocopy any of it. I came across the section where Merton wrote of his conversion experience. He said it was so moving that he frequently found himself in tears, even at the moment he was writing. "The tears," he wrote, "are actually falling on the page of my notebook." And there it was right before me, the writings of Merton smudged by his tears.

Over a period of years, a real change occurred in Merton from the Roman Catholic monk of the *Seven Storey Mountain* to the Christian pilgrim of the *Asian Journal*. The earlier Merton was one who lived in the security of post–World War II America and the pre–Vatican II Roman Catholic Church. All was very secure. Certitude ruled the day. His autobiography reflects this attitude. The monastic rule and the bell were *Vox Dei* (The Voice of God) for Merton. He lived by these rules day in and day out. He was the good monk.

Merton was deeply human and very much felt the social pain of the 1960s. Many of his writings, such as *Conjectures of a Guilty Bystander,* reveal a tremendous sensitivity to the key issues of our day: economic injustices, war, racism, sexism, ecclesiastical politics. Merton's spirituality now embraced the entire world. He wasn't simply the quiet little monk in his monastery. His voice was heard loudly and clearly among those who gathered to wrestle with the social ills of our day.

Merton gradually realized that he was connected with all humankind, that being a monk did not place him in an isolated social class. He also started to realize that Roman Catholics did not have a monopoly on God. To come to a deeper understanding of God, we need to join hands with people of all races and creeds. He wrote in *Mystics and Zen Masters:*

Our task now is to learn that if we can voyage to the ends of the earth and there find ourselves in the aborigine who most differs from ourselves, we will have made a fruitful pilgrimage. That is why pilgrimage is necessary, in some shape or other. Mere sitting at home and meditating on the divine presence is not enough for our time. We have come to the end of a long journey and see that the stranger we meet there is no other than ourselves, which is the same as saying that we find Christ in him.[13]

The Merton that we know as a human being was transformed by his experience of change. The first major shift took place in Rome, where he prayed for the first time in his life. The Byzantine mosaics there inspired him. He discovered the stunning mosaic of Christ the Pantocrator. That artistic rendering of the Lord of Glory profoundly affected the youthful Merton. It yielded his first real insight into Christianity. "And now for the first time in my life I began to find out something of who this person was that men called Christ. It was there that I first saw him, whom now I serve as my God and King, and who owns and rules my life. It is the Christ of the apocalypse, the Christ of the Fathers. It is Christ the King."[14] This experience, mediated by a symbol, was eventually to lead Merton to the monastery, where his initial response would be to follow the traditional ascetical methods to reach personal sanctification.

The second transforming experience was quite different and occurred after Merton had been a monk for a number of years. "In Louisville, at the corner of Fourth and Walnut, I was suddenly overwhelmed with the realization that I loved all those people, that they were mine and I theirs, that we could not be alien to one another even though we were total strangers. The whole illusion of a separate holy existence is a dream."[15] Here the context of religious experience and its symbols reaches a significant expansion in Merton's life.

Merton continued to think about the Christ whom he first discovered in Byzantine art. His experience kept on enriching and changing his view of this Christ. In a talk given toward the end of his life in Calcutta on the feast of Christ the King, he asked

> What is the meaning of Christ the King? To recognize Christ as King, it is not enough to recognize him as a kind of leader who is somewhere off in space and looking down from a kind of head office. Christ is King enthroned in our hearts. Christ is King but he does not control by power; further he does not control by law. Christ is King but he controls by love. This love is the very root of my own being. Who am I? My deepest realization of who I am is — I am one loved by Christ.[16]

Just as Thomas Merton's initial religious experience was occasioned by an artistic symbol, so was his final one. Just a few days before he died, he encountered some statues of Buddha in a garden of Ceylon. He wrote of this experience:

> I am able to approach the Buddhas barefoot and undisturbed. I was knocked over with a rush of relief and thankfulness at the obvious charity of the figures. Looking at these figures I was suddenly, almost forcibly jerked clean out of the habitual, half-tied vision of things.... All problems are resolved and everything is clear, simply because what matters is clear. I don't know when in my life I have ever had such a sense of beauty and spiritual validity running together in one aesthetic illumination.[17]

At this point in his life, Merton reached the height of a universal mystical outlook and experience. In his first encounter with the Byzantine risen Christ, his deepest yearning and impulse was to repent and review his disordered life. In the case of the Buddhas of Polonnaruwa, the image of freely enlightened human peace confirmed the intuition garnered by Merton's experience of Christian mysticism through the years. His discovery was that the extraordinary character of the ordinary and the charged presence of the divine is in everything that is.

His life became one of self-transcendence and communion. Merton ultimately discovered that the choice is not between

God and human beings. The choice is a daily decision to find God through loving others. He wrote, "It is love for my lover, my child, my brother, that enables me to show God to them. Love is the epiphany of God in our poverty."[18] Merton became a mystic because he finally saw the connection between all things.

Although each of us has to be faithful on the journey as we experience it, Merton is a model for us. Just as changing times forced Abraham and Sarah to reshape their dreams, Thomas Merton learned to become comfortable with the fact that there were more questions than answers in his life. For him, God was in the questions. On the eve of a new millennium, as a culture and church we find ourselves wandering on the Emmaus Road. If we open our eyes, we will discover the Lord and one another in new and unexpected places.

Today's Christian is challenged to let go of the security of former days. For us, God is in the insecurity. This is the rude awakening that has been going on in our church and country for the past thirty years. Are we willing to become pilgrims, traveling to new places, reshaping our dreams, and being led by God's spirit wherever that might be? God is in the journey. May Merton's prayer energize us along the way!

My Lord God, I have no idea where I am going. I do not see the road ahead of me. I cannot know for certain where it will end. Nor do I really know myself, and the fact that I think that I am following your will does not mean that I am actually doing so. But I believe that the desire to please you does in fact please you. And I hope I have that desire in all that I am doing. I hope that I will never do anything apart from that desire. And I know that if I do this you will lead me by the right road though I may know nothing about it. Therefore will I trust you always though I may seem to be lost and in the shadow of death. I will never fear, for you are ever with me, and you will never leave me to face my perils alone.[19]

Conclusion

Although we long for stability, holiness and spiritual growth are often found in change. The biblical paradigm for life's journey is one of constant repentance, conversion, and modification. Contemporary developmental theories support this viewpoint. The saints and mystics often wrote about the spiritual life as being a journey and a process. The human person is in a state of constant flux.

Life in the marketplace today is far from secure and certain. Inner strength and peace are more essential today than ever before. Mastering the developmental stages through an openness to God's grace is the way to holiness. People who come to terms with who they are at different stages of life bring a serenity and integrity into everyday life.

This view of spirituality is one that admits different needs and expressions of prayer at different times in one's life. To be truly holy, then, should find us different today than we were yesterday. And the holy person will refuse to rest in today's security, for tomorrow's holiness will re-create us once again.

The developmental process of growth and holiness rests on a deep rooted faith and trust in God:

> Look at the birds in the sky. They do not sow or reap, they gather nothing into barns; yet your heavenly Father feeds them. Are you not worth more than they? Which of you by worrying can add a moment to his life-span?...O weak in faith! Stop worrying....Your Heavenly Father knows all that you need. Seek first his reign over you, his way of holiness and all these things will be given you besides. Enough, then, of worrying about tomorrow. Let tomorrow take care of itself. Today has troubles enough of its own. (Matt. 6:26–34)

REFLECTION STARTERS

1. Spend some time reflecting on your life. Draw a line and divide your life into five-year periods. Write whatever experiences come to mind from each period, both positive and negative. Spend some time in prayer, thanking God for the good moments and trying to get in touch with any unfinished business, questions, hurts, or failures. Draw up a list of the things you need to work on. Bring these to prayer, spiritual direction, counseling, or a trusted friend.

2. Review the dreams and goals of your life. Spend some time mourning over those that are unfulfilled and think about ways that you might reshape your dreams.

3. Think of someone you know who might be experiencing a serious life transition at this time. What are some ways that you might be supportive? Challenging?

4. How do you feel about the transitional times we're now experiencing in the churches and our culture? Try to identify these feelings, whether happy, sad, fearful, or anxious. Share your thoughts and opinions on what you think your individual contribution and our collective mission as a church should be during these times.

5. What do you think of Thomas Merton as a model? Who has been a model or mentor for you on your journey?

CHAPTER THREE

Writing Straight with Crooked Lines

This is Daddy's bedtime secret for today: Man is born broken, He lives by mending. The grace of God is glue.
— EUGENE O'NEILL, *The Great God Brown*

FOCUS QUESTIONS

- Does God cause suffering?

- Would you prefer a life without suffering?

- Think of an example where suffering made you bitter. How could you have dealt with the pain differently? Is it possible that you could have become wise instead of bitter through this experience?

Why Suffering?

Pain and suffering are not strangers to any of us. We meet them all along the way of life's stages of development. If we are to grow and change, we must die to ourselves. This necessarily entails pain. This reality is clearly reflected in nature. The seed must die for the plant to grow. Ice must melt to become usable as water. The atom must be split for energy to emerge. To bring this even closer to home, look to your personal experience. You had to suffer the trauma of leaving your mother's womb to enter the world. Again you had to die to self to leave the world of childhood for adolescence and again from adolescence to adulthood.

Suffering is a part of life. All suffering has the potential of being growth-producing. Suffering as a way of life or as an end itself has no value. Whenever my father would see one of us children wallowing in self-pity, he would smile and say, "Get off the cross; we need the wood." We can become so engrossed in suffering that we can forget that in itself suffering is an evil.

One day St. Teresa of Avila was riding along in a carriage. When she got out of the carriage, she slipped on a rock and fell head-on into a mud puddle. Standing up, habit full of dirt, she raised her eyes to the sky and said, "God, if you treat your friends this way, no wonder you have so few of them!" Does God really treat friends this way? Does God cause suffering? Do the Gospels really teach "No pain, no gain?" In these transitional times our explanations for the universal experience of pain need to be revisited. In this chapter, I will deal with the roots of our negative understanding of suffering. A new spirituality of suffering needs to be articulated in light of new theological and psychological developments.

Because some have accepted traditional beliefs about suffering, they sometimes have harshly interpreted God and human existence. Their conviction that pain for pain's sake is a value has often led them to an unhealthy introversion and great fear of an angry God. This is not to deny that suffering can indirectly be a blessing to the degree that it leads to human development and spiritual growth.

I have never been attracted to negative portrayals of suffering. Even in the second grade this model of suffering repulsed me. I remember Sr. Fidelis announcing that the communists would be coming soon. "In fact," she said, "they will be arriving any day." She told us, "The first place they would go is the church, and they will want to get into the tabernacle. Under no circumstances," she said, "are you to give them the key. They will cut off your fingers and chop off your legs, but don't give them the key. Be a martyr for the faith." I remember suddenly feeling nauseated. I raised my hand and said, "Sister, where is the key?" She asked, "Why do you want to know?" I responded, "Just in case I don't want my fingers and legs cut off." I got in big trouble for that remark.

The notion that God wants us to suffer always bothered me. God does not will suffering. In fact, it is Catholic teaching that suffering was not part of God's original plan for the world. God did not create suffering. It is the result of our choice for sin. Even before I studied theology, my gut told me that there was something wrong with our notion of suffering. For example, when I arrived at the seminary, a friend had left a gift on my desk. It was a book with a red cover inscribed with the word SUFFERING in big black letters. I instinctively knew that to seek suffering as a goal was not sound. People often thought it was virtuous to inflict painful, senseless rules to subdue sinful human nature. This kind of suffering is not good because it denies that human nature is essentially good.

Jansenistic Roots

Recently I was making a retreat at a monastery, truly a peaceful place. One day I was taking a walk through the monastery gardens. Suddenly I was jolted from my mellow mood when I saw a huge concrete crucifix. Jesus looked severe. In huge letters beneath the cross were carved the words, "I suffered for you. What are you now doing for me?" That's a graphic illustration of a Jansenistic spirituality. The underlying message of this crucifix is that it was God's will that Jesus suffer. Now it's our turn to suffer for our sins.

The belief that suffering is good in itself and that it is our lot in life to suffer is rooted in Jansenism. This heresy flourished in seventeenth- and eighteenth-century France. Cornelius Jansen, professor of Scripture at Louvain and bishop of Ypres, spearheaded this movement. In his book *Augustinus* he taught that Adam and Eve lost their freedom after the fall and were completely motivated by concupiscence. This negative view about the corruption of human nature taught that the body was evil and needed to be subdued. Only the less virtuous would give in to the desire to marry. Even legitimate intercourse was considered a venial sin. This belief system suggested that people were predestined. They could do absolutely nothing to reverse the divine plan.

Jansenism was introduced into France by Jean Duvergier de Hauranne, abbot of Saint-Cyran. Antoine Arnuald, priest and teacher at the Sorbonne, taught the Jansenistic doctrine of grace and introduced this spirituality to the Convent of Port-Royal. The nuns practiced a severe asceticism, which included whippings and being nailed to crosses. Because they saw themselves as sinful they would adore the Eucharist but rarely receive communion. The expression of emotions, especially any kind of affection, was to be avoided at all costs.[1] This was carried so far that Jansenists were even forbidden to hug their children or to cry at the funeral of a loved one.

The spiritual retreats given at Port-Royal were heavily responsible for the spread of Jansenism throughout France. They preached that even the righteous could be damned. To seek any kind of pleasure, even legitimate entertainment such as the theater and concerts, was forbidden. Jansenists taught that especially in solitude we must do penance because the devil will severely tempt people during times of prayer. This Jansenistic obsession with perfection drove some people to despair. One always had to be on guard. Even relaxation was viewed as a concession to human weakness.

Jansenism made its way into the bloodstream of the church. Irish seminarians were indoctrinated into Jansenistic teachings in France. They brought Jansenism home to Ireland, where it was received wholeheartedly. The Irish missionaries then carried these tenets to the Irish immigrants to America. For the next two hundred years, well into the twentieth century, Jansenism set the tone for American Catholic spirituality.

A severe, rigid spirituality emerged from these premises. A degrading humility that saturated Catholic behavior for centuries became its cornerstone. The following true anecdote illustrates the point. In the 1950s, Brother Damian went to his novice master, Fr. Dismas, and said, "Father, you make me feel like two cents." Dismas responded by saying, "Well, brother, I haven't succeeded yet because you are supposed to feel like nothing." Dismas ended his admonition by saying, "And besides, the two cents is a sin against poverty." This story is typically Jansenistic in its stress on inflicted pain and suffering as the way to spiritual growth. Until very recently most people in our culture sincerely believed and practiced a spirituality that was heavily rooted in Jansenistic values.

To Love Is to Suffer

The notion of suffering long predates the twisted turn of Jansenism. It transcends the Judeo-Christian experience because suffering and pain are universal human experiences. This theme fills the pages of the New Testament. The crucified Christ is a positive model for all those who suffer. St. Paul wrote that "God shows his love for us in that while we were still sinners, Christ died for us" (Rom. 5:8). The kind of love that is totally selfless is called *agapē*. This is what Jesus models on the cross. He loved us and gave us an example through his self-surrender. Christ's suffering was motivated by love and brought life to others.

The early Christian community espoused this kind of love. The Acts of the Apostles tells the story of the love that early Christians had for one another, especially in their sharing and living in common. St. Paul's goal was always to build up communities of love. The first Christians healthily translated the suffering of the cross into love of neighbor.

As a young boy, I hero-worshiped Fr. Mark. He was a strong, sensitive person. I didn't realize that he had suffered a series of nervous breakdowns. While he was at our parish, he took the youth group on a bus trip. He corrected Skip for yelling out the bus window. Skip challenged him to a fist fight. We were all shocked. Of course, Fr. Mark did not fight with Skip. All the way home on the bus, Skip kept calling him a "yellow-bellied chicken." This precipitated another nervous breakdown, a transfer from our parish, and his eventual resignation from the active ministry.

Fr. Mark moved back to Italy, his birthplace. I hadn't heard from him in many years. He wrote to me for my ordination, and shared his story.

> I was committed to mental hospitals in 1972 and 1973. Before that I had been committed five times, starting in 1963. I was considered a nonrecuperable patient in 1972. At that moment a woman entered into my life, when I had been transferred to an inner ward where the patients stay practically for the rest of their lives. Her name is Ann. She thought that a big injustice had been done with me and that I would really turn completely insane if I stayed there much longer. She began visiting me daily, bringing me books and writing me letters. She did this after working eight hours a day and doing extra duties as a private nurse. Because of the wear and tear on her, her family and friends told her to stop visiting me. Thank God, she didn't. Because of her I am a well man and happy today.

Ann's gift of love saved Mark. She is a cogent example of what it means to die to self for the sake of others. Because of her love, Mark now has new life and a hope-filled future. She shared Mark's suffering. She gave him *agapē*. This is what Jesus did in his suffering on the cross. All true love includes some suffering. The very nature of love, the total self-giving to others, necessitates a holy suffering, modeled on Christ, who suffered for the love of humankind. This is *agapē,* the highest form of love, the greatest gift of all (1 Cor. 13:13).

Martyrdom

The early Christian communities believed that another way of living *agapē* was to accept the martyrdom that was inflicted upon them in the Roman persecutions during the first three centuries. Many of these men and women courageously accepted death as an expression of their love of God and neighbor. These people were true witnesses to the power of love and the strength of faith.

There are three accounts of martyrdom in Scripture: that of Eleazar and the seven brothers in 2 Maccabees 6:18–7:41, of Stephen in Acts 6:8–7:60, and of Christ on the cross. These became models for Christians during the persecutions. The first writings of the Fathers of the Church were about the suffering of martyrdom. They presented a positive view of the heroic suffering so many endured. Martyrdom was seen in the context of discipleship and love of neighbor. The following is typical of what motivated these men and women:

> We could never abandon Christ, for it was he who suffered for the redemption of those who are saved in the entire world, the innocent one dying on behalf of sinners. Nor could we worship anyone else. For him we reverence as the Son of God, whereas we love the martyrs as the disciples and imitators of the Lord, and rightly so because of their unsurpassed loyalty towards their king and master. May we too share with them as fellow disciples.[2]

The earliest account of the martyrdom of Polycarp, written in the second century, reflects the communion with God and neighbor felt by the first martyrs: "I sacrifice myself for you, Ephesians. My spirit sacrifices itself for you, not only now, but when I shall attain God."[3] This spirit of communion experienced in martyrdom so filled the spirit of the early churches that it became a permanent component in Christian spirituality for future ages.

In the third century, Origen used the image of the Christian life as a pilgrimage. His thinking was that life is a cumulative series of self-denials in preparation for the ultimate goal of physical martyrdom. Just as Christ's death brought redemption to the world, so too the sacrifice of the martyr brought life to the community.[4]

The early accounts of the death of martyrs stress two characteristics of these men and women. The first was an ecstasy in which they became so absorbed in their desire for martyrdom as a way to God that they transcended the physical pain of the torture. The second was a deep awareness and insight into the culture. Their way of responding to the decadence of their society was to transcend it by their martyrdom.[5]

A later emphasis on the ecstasy model led to an obsession with the details of physical martyrdom. The following is a typical account:

> The Blessed Blandina was last of all: like a noble mother encouraging her children she hastened to rejoin them, rejoicing and glorifying in her death as though she had been invited to a bridal banquet instead of being the victim of the beasts. After the scourges, the animals, and the hot griddle, she was at last tossed into a net and exposed to a bull. After being tossed a good deal by the animal, she no longer perceived what was happening because of the hope and possession of all she believed in and because of her intimacy with Christ.[6]

Books on the lives of the saints emphasized this kind of detailed account of the physical dimensions of martyrdom. They emphasized the asceticism of martyrdom instead of the prophetic awareness that martyrs brought to the church and the world.

Although the actual period of martyrdom ended with the Edict of Milan in 313, the spirit of martyrdom was too deeply rooted in the Christian psyche to ever be eliminated. It became the model for Christian sanctity. In fact, the end of physical martyrdom created a void in the church. Monasticism emerged in response to people's need to live differently from the surrounding culture. The life of the monk was to be a spiritual martyrdom. Monasticism was labelled "white martyrdom" as contrasted to "red" physical martyrdom.

The eventual weakening of the church's spirituality of martyrdom led to severe and inhuman ascetical practices. Later spiritual manuals and developments in religious life valued the pain of martyrdom as an end itself. In a sense, Jansenism was a theology of martyrdom gone wild. Much of our thinking about suffering is rooted in this later development in the theology of martyrdom and in Jansenism, more than it is in the Gospel of Jesus Christ and the initial understanding of martyrdom that centered on *agapē*. The challenge for today's spirituality is to rediscover the positive aspects of early Christian martyrdom's notion of suffering. The early martyrs aimed for intimacy with God, a life-giving dependence on other human beings, and a prophetic awareness about the needs of the church and the world.

An Age-Old Mystery

Life is not fair. It is natural to ask "Why" when we experience pain, suffering, or bad luck. Jansenism and an unhealthy spirituality of martyrdom have left many questions about suffering unanswered.

The fact that we never stop asking why came home to me when some friends who are devout Catholics went to the casinos in Atlantic City. They lost $500 playing Blackjack. They were with another couple who are staunch atheists. This couple won $800 that same night. My friends called me when they got home. "How come," they asked, "we who are religious and moral people lose and our atheist friends win? It just doesn't seem fair." At first I laughed at their question. But the more I thought about it, the more I realized that their problem is an age-old mystery. It was really the question the Jews asked in the Hebrew Scriptures. The traditional belief was that good people were rewarded and that bad people were punished with suffering and bad luck in this life.

Actually, their question came to my mind this year when I was at Yad Vashem, Israel's Holocaust Museum. I was deeply depressed after walking through the museum. The architects truly succeed in giving the viewer a glimpse of the horror of the Holocaust. Especially poignant was the senseless suffering of little children. The intensity of the pain and brutal deaths of six million Jews was powerfully conveyed.

After walking through the museum, I went outside and stood

before a modernistic statue of Job. He was holding his hands to his head in despair and utter desperation. I was disturbed by the statue. It evoked feelings of desperation and hopelessness. Job is a powerful symbol of the senselessness and cruelty of inflicted human suffering.

Do yourself a favor: reread the book of Job. It deals with life's most basic questions. Your first impression might be that it is a sad story. When I was a deacon on my first assignment, I was stationed with a priest who had been just one year ahead of me in the seminary. Chris was an intense person. When we visited the hospital, he would give patients the book of Job. One day the pastor said to me, "What's he doing that for? He should be giving out books about Snoopy and Charlie Brown to cheer people up!" What the pastor didn't realize is that the conclusion of the book of Job is very cheery, upbeat, and optimistic. Although the book of Job is heavy reading in parts, its teachings about God and human life are ultimately optimistic. In the end, Job's health and family are restored to him.

Job, a pious and upright chieftain, rich in money, property, and popularity, suffers an abrupt and complete reversal of fortune. He loses his money, property, and family. He is afflicted with a frightful disease. Three friends come to visit, armed with Israel's prevalent understanding of suffering. They tell him that God is punishing him for some wrongdoing. Israel's belief up to that point was that the good prospered and the wicked suffered. Having grown up with these beliefs, Job anguishes over these questions and demands an explanation from God, since he in fact has done nothing wrong to deserve this punishment.

Try to imagine the depth of despair Job experienced. It is very characteristic of our contemporary experience. Just today I received an interesting advertisement. On the front of the envelope above my name and address in large blue letters was written, "Uneasy about the church? Worried about the country?" In today's world much of life is lived between two moods, anxiety and high anxiety. The tension is reminiscent of Job's struggle: "I cry to you, but you do not answer me. My harp is turned to mourning. But what is our lot from God above?

This is my final plea; let the Almighty answer me" (30:20, 31; 31:2, 37).

Job examines his conscience to understand what he did to deserve such awful torment. He feels utterly hopeless and confused. He demands an explanation from God. The wealth of Israel's wisdom tradition was no longer satisfying. Something was missing in the traditional explanation of pain.

Chapter 38 of the book of Job is one of the Bible's most sublime passages. God overwhelms Job with the splendor of creation and asks one question: "By what right do you ask me to give an account of myself?" Job simply prostrates himself in adoration. This was the most appropriate response after hearing such touching words from God:

> Where were you when I founded the earth? ... Have you ever in your lifetime commanded the morning and shown the dawn its place? ... Have you entered into the sources of the sea, or walked about in the depths of the abyss? ... Who counts the clouds in his wisdom? Or who tilts the water jars of heaven so that the dust of earth is fused into a mass and its cods made solid? ... Does the eagle fly up at your command to build his nest aloft? ... Will we have arguing with the Almighty by the critic? Let him who would correct God give answer! (Job 38: 4, 12, 16, 37–38; 39:27; 40:2)

Job responds, "Behold, I am of little account, what can I answer you? I put my hand over my mouth" (Job 40:4). Job's faith is deepened. He now realizes that Israel's explanations for suffering pale before the mystery of God: "I know that you can do all things, and that no purpose of yours can be hindered. I have dealt with great things I do not understand; things too wonderful for me, which I cannot know" (Job 42:2–3). The God who has created the world loves his creation too much to cause it pain. God does not cause suffering, but allows it to occur. The question of "Why suffering?" is never really answered. The point of the story is that good things, such as the deepening of faith and becoming comfortable with mystery, can result from suffering. God doesn't cause suffering, yet suffering can be a pathway to deeper growth in understanding ourselves, loving God, and reaching out to our neighbors. It's what St. Augustine meant when he wrote, "God writes straight with crooked lines."[7]

No More Pastries

Suffering happens in many ways. Often emotional pain is far more severe than physical suffering. Take, for example, the feeling of emptiness. Most people loathe this experience. Everything deteriorates and nothing makes sense. Our world seems to fall apart. It is a Job experience. In times like these, we feel alone. Even God and friends are no consolation.

This triggers a series of events. Emptiness leads to depression, tiredness, and helplessness. Anxiety comes from everything in general and nothing in particular. There seems to be no purpose to life. We are impatient with ourselves for being stuck in this rut. Everything seems gloomy.

We can devise ways to escape emptiness. Workaholism, alcoholism, drugs, sexual aberrations, overeating, and oversleeping are possible choices. The irony is that these options generally create a deeper void. They might bring momentary relief, but ultimately they worsen the condition.

Another possibility is to accept the emptiness, without judging or fighting the experience. We need some solitude and space to feel the feeling, consider the meaning of the experience, and understand what options are available. If we do this, healthy paths are more likely. Deeper relationships might occur. We can more deeply appreciate others and be ready for *agapē* love.

And then there's depression, a part of everyone's life. Sharp depression indicates that something is absent in our lives. The temptation is to deal only with the symptom. Depression generally signals that something needs to change. To deal with the change, one has to discover the root of the depression. This takes time and hard work.

Facing the anxiety can be energizing. It can lead us to

seek support or involvement with larger communities such as churches, political parties, or self-help groups like Alcoholics Anonymous or Overeaters Anonymous. It can be a time of abandoning old notions of God and embracing new images. Recognizing our need for God and others can be a time of breathtaking beginnings.

Dealing with emptiness can lead to a fuller life. Significant life changes can result from these painful experiences. St. Teresa of Avila taught that our avoidance of the cross due to fear of the darkness prevents progress in our human development. She lived with the feeling of emptiness and darkness for sixteen years. The temptation, she taught, is to run from the darkness. Her experience of deep intimacy with God in prayer after many years of living with the darkness gives us hope that there is light at the end of the tunnel if we stay with the empty feelings caused by suffering.[8]

I remember a dream I had about Italian pastries. I love pastries. Every imaginable pastry was in the dream. I was ecstatic. In the middle of the dream, the Lord came and said, "You love these pastries, don't you?" I answered, "I sure do!" And Jesus said, "That's your problem: you always want pastries." Emptiness is living without pastries for a while, so that we can move to bigger and better things. That's precisely the good that can come out of suffering. It eventually brings growth in self-knowledge and deeper relationships with God and others. To run from this opportunity is reminiscent of the rich young man in the Gospel: " 'You are lacking one thing. Go sell what you have, and give to the poor and you will have treasure in heaven; then come, follow me.' At that statement his face fell, and he went away sad, for he had many possessions" (Mark 10:21–22). Rejecting the opportunity to let go during times of emptiness is to miss the chance of a lifetime and to walk away very sad, falling even deeper into the well of emptiness.

If we are really going to grow, we eventually have to let go of the certainties and defense mechanisms that protect us from real love. For many years, I was a workaholic. This shielded me from the pain of emptiness. I was rewarded with much praise and respect because of my hard work. Most people reinforced my avoidance of emptiness.

But deep down inside, I knew I was running away. At the age of forty-one, I began to feel anxiety that I couldn't shake anymore. I began to question many things about God, the church, the world, and even myself. I questioned much of what I had been taught. I suddenly had more questions than answers. I can still remember going to my superior and saying, "I need to go for therapy." He looked shocked. I was perceived as one of the more together people in ministry. I knew he didn't understand what I was telling him.

This was the beginning of the four roughest years of my life. Everything fell apart. I didn't know who God was, what I was about, why I belonged to the church, or what I was supposed to do in the world. I didn't know what I felt or what I really thought. Through the therapeutic process, I began to feel my feelings of love, anger, fear, sexual attraction, and anxiety. For a while, I didn't want to have anything to do with God, the church, and even some close friends. I felt that it was all a lie, and I was angry.

I walked in the "valley of darkness" for a long time. I kept wishing that it would be all over, that there would be a quick solution, and that I wouldn't feel this way anymore. But it continued.

This was a time of grace for me. It was learning to live without the pastries for the first time in my life. All the props were removed. God finally had a chance to break into my life. It was the real beginning of the spiritual journey. I had to discover a God whom I had never met. I had to develop a relationship and learn how to converse with this God. I had to redefine the church and my place in it. Most difficult of all, I had to learn how to love people and allow them to love me. The agony of emptiness led me to a fuller and more meaningful life. The very pain that I ran from all those years was the key to my salvation. Staying with the emptiness of my inner tombs for four years brought about a wonderful resurrection in my life.

To Be with Those Who Suffer

Dealing with pain creatively can change us for the better and can make us more understanding of the suffering of others. Christ did not suffer for the sake of suffering. His suffering and ultimate rejection resulted from his deep involvement with people, especially sinners and outcasts. He was crucified because his choices challenged the political, economic, and religious structures of his time. His sufferings brought salvation, freedom, and new life to the despondent. His suffering had value because it brought redemption and life to others.

Christ recognized that the suffering that comes from oppression is evil. Like Christ, we must do what we can to alleviate this kind of pain. We must challenge systems and structures that cause this kind of anguish and deprivation. We should embrace as our special friends those who suffer due to injustices.

The Catholic Church publicly committed itself to addressing these issues when it shifted its option from the middle class to the poor and suffering of the world. The church has come full circle in its social teaching. Pope Pius IX taught the poor and oppressed that their social and economic status was their vocation, and it was a sin to try to change it. Pope Leo XIII encouraged Christians to endure and suffer injustices for the sake of the greater good. At the same time he challenged the economic order and called the power structures to a greater charity toward the poor. With few variations, this was the teaching of the popes up to Pope John XXIII. His teachings about peace and the sharing of economic goods paved the way for some radical shifts in social doctrine. He began to turn the page in the book of the church's social doctrine.

Pope Paul VI boldly carried this teaching even further. He proposed a transformation of the economic order. He went so far as to concede that violence might be justified in extreme cases to bring about social changes. Pope John Paul II continued this progressive social direction. He confronted all oppressive systems in both the East and West. For the first time in centuries the church definitively moved away from favoring the rich and middle class to favoring the poor, marginated, and oppressed.[9]

The spirituality of martyrdom has been renewed. Insertion among the oppressed and solidarity with suffering is today's martyrdom. Archbishop Oscar Romero and the countless other victims who have died in developing countries for the poor are powerful models of a contemporary martyrdom. In this spirituality, martyrs are the ones who unmask the system; that is why they suffer its violence. Jesus himself did not remain indifferent to suffering's victims. He became poor and was condemned and crucified in communion with all who suffer rejection and oppression. When the sons of Zebedee asked Jesus for positions of power in his kingdom, Jesus responded, "Are you able to drink the cup that I drink?" (Matt. 20:20–28), as if to say: Can you suffer what I am going to suffer? Then he summoned the Twelve and informed them that whoever would be first must be the servant of the rest, offering himself as an example: "For the Son of Man also came not to be served but to serve, and to give his life as a ransom for many" (Matt. 20:28). Laying down one's life through service is to be in union with the poor and suffering.

This came together for me several years ago when I was in the South Bronx participating in a workshop on the *Spiritual Exercises* of St. Ignatius of Loyola. When we got to the Third Week of the Exercises about the passion of Christ, the directors told us to take the day to reflect on the sufferings and death of our Lord. Docile student that I am, I went Bible in hand and spent the day in the chapel. I looked up all the passion accounts in the Gospels. I reflected on my personal experience of the cross. I then divided my life down into five-year intervals to review my history of suffering.

At the end of the day, we all gathered in the conference room to share our reflections. I shared the parallels in my life to the passion. A Jesuit in our group had had a very different experience. He had spent the day walking the streets of the Bronx, getting in touch with the sufferings of the poor and oppressed. It was here that he encountered the crucified Christ. The passion of Christ came alive for him. I suddenly felt embarrassed. My reflection on suffering was introspective. There's nothing wrong with that in itself, except that it is not enough. Jesus died because he preached the Reign of God and identified with sinners and tax collectors. In his sufferings on Calvary, he experienced intense pain, which led him to look to the Father and to embrace all of us in his supreme act of love. He models for us the path of redemptive suffering. This kind of suffering moves beyond introspection and enters into the experience of the poor and oppressed.

Another Jesuit told a moving story of what it means to identify with the suffering Christ in today's world. His friend Jack was a medical examiner. One night he got a call from the police to go to an apartment in Westchester where a young woman had died. When he got there, a middle-aged couple pointed to where the body was. When he went into the room, he said that he was shocked. He had never seen a body like this one before. The body was immaculately clean. It was a female only four feet tall, stretched out and beautifully dressed. Jack knew that there was something different about this case.

After Jack had examined the body, he said to the couple, "Why didn't you call me two days ago?" The man responded, "This was our niece. She was nineteen years old. My sister gave birth to her out of wedlock. She was born twisted. At the time, the doctors told us that she would be blind, mute, and deaf." He then told Jack that his sister was unable to keep the baby. She was unfit emotionally and incapable financially of taking on such a great responsibility. James and his wife decided to take the baby. For nineteen years, they took care of her, changing her diapers three times a day. At first they took the girl out, but too many people stared at them. Friends even stopped visiting them because it was too painful to watch this little girl.

James and Kathy continued, "But we loved her, and she knew it. When she died three days ago, we thought that her limbs would go stiff and then would relax. We hoped to see her twisted body relaxed for the first time in nineteen years. But it didn't happen. We then took her body and began bathing it in the bathtub and anointing her with oil. Her body was finally limp. We went out and found the most beautiful gown we could buy, dressed her, and then called the police."

On a recent trip to Rome, I noticed how deeply moving Michelangelo's *Pietà* really is. Mary is holding the suffering Christ. She does not look at him, but rather at us, as if to say, "Come, share his pain." The Jesuit who walked the streets of the South Bronx and James and Kathy experienced the Christ who suffers today. True spirituality is to move beyond our own pain and to feel and be with those who suffer in our world.

Today's Lepers

The leper stories in the life of St. Francis are intriguing. It was his embracing of lepers that was at the heart of his conversion. His personal identity in God was found by embracing lepers. His experience is a paradigm for today's spiritual journey. Where are today's lepers and how can they lead us to God? Certainly, James and Kathy found Christ in their niece. She was their leper and their way to God.

It would be worthwhile to unravel the thirteenth-century leper stories in the life of St. Francis to understand their powerful relevance for today. Leprosy then was not only a physical disease but also a social and spiritual one. As in the time of Job, it was thought that leprosy was a punishment for sin.

Lepers hid until someone reported them. They were dragged from their houses to the church. They were beat up and thrown in front of the altar. A religious ritual was performed that actually separated them forever from the human race. The horrible ritual captured the hostility that people had toward lepers. It nauseates me to think that human beings could be treated in this way. This treatment of humans did not end in the thirteenth century, of course. As you read the following description of the leprosy ritual, think of people today living with AIDS:

> It was a rainy evening near the end of November. All the candles were lit. In the shadows, some objects were dimly seen on a table at the side of the sacristy door. The church

was filled with the devout, curious, pious. The bell rang. The priest came out in cope and stole, preceded by clerics carrying the cross. He went up the steps of the altar, turned, and with the same gesture he used at funerals, sprinkled with holy water the leper who was about to die to the world. Then he delivered his admonition:

"My brothers, dear poor little man of good God, by means of great sadness and tribulation, of sickness, of leprosy, and of many other miseries, one gains the kingdom of heaven, where there is no sickness or sorrow. All is pure and white, without stain, more brilliant than the sun. You will go there, if it pleases God. In the meantime, be a good Christian, bear with patience this adversity, and God will be merciful to you."

The terrible words fell into a silence as profound as the silence of a cemetery. The living corpse bent still lower to the ground. He seemed to be looking for his grave.

"My brother, the separation has to do only with your body. As for the spirit, which is more important, you are still, as you were before, a participant in the prayers of our Holy Mother Church, as if every day you were assisting in the Divine Offices. Charitable men will provide for your lesser needs, and God will never abandon you. Take care of yourself and have patience. God is with you. Amen."

From the hands of the acolyte the celebrant took a handful of black earth brought from the nearby cemetery; he sprinkled it on the head of the sick man.

"Die to the world, be born again in God. O Jesus my redeemer, who made me of earth and clothed me with a body, make me to rise again in the new day."

The priest continued, "My brother, take this cloak and put it on in sign of humility and never leave here without it." Reluctantly the leper put it on. It is the ominous uniform that will make everyone he meets flee from him.

"Take this little flask. Put in it what will be given you to drink, and under penalty of disobedience I forbid you to drink from the rivers, from the springs, from the wells. Take these gloves. You are forbidden to touch anything that is not yours with your bare hands."

The priest continued, "If, while walking about, you should meet someone who wishes to talk to you, I forbid you to reply before you put yourself against the wind. You are forbidden to be with any woman who is not of your family. You are forbidden to touch young people or to offer them anything. And from eating from anything but your own leper's bowl. And from entering churches or rectories, and from going to fairs, to mills, and to markets. And from walking through narrow streets where those who meet you cannot avoid you."

At last he was given the wooden clapper, the kind sounded in Holy Week.

"Take this tentennella; carry it always with you. Sound it to warn others of your presence."

A cortege formed as if the body was to be accompanied to a cemetery, the cross in front, then the clerics, the priest, the leper, the faithful. Night had fallen. The enclosure reeked of a sad autumnal fever. The tentennella, shaken by the leper, filled the air with its dismal, clear sound. The flames of the candles threw light along the long corridors and narrow passages, on the high columns. The procession seemed to be passing through a walled cemetery, amid deathlike odors of dampnesss and decay.

The cell was ready. A wooden cross was on the door. The ghost entered the cell with his gravedigger. Inside were a low, mean bed, like a bier, a table, a chair, a lamp, and a strong box. An attendant handed the newcomer sandals, a camelskin hood, an earthenware pot, a beechwood bowl, a copper jug, a belt, a knife. Everything else the leper owned went to the hospital of the commune.

Now he was required to make the proper response:

"Here is my perpetual resting place. Here I shall live. This is my vow."

The priest said the concluding prayer:

"Omnipotent God, who throws down the pride of the ancient enemy through the sufferings of your only Son, give to your servant the necessary strength to bear with devotion and patience the evil that oppresses him."[10]

Reading this awful description, it is understandable that anyone living in the thirteenth century would have little or no use for lepers. Before his conversion, St. Francis was like everyone else is his attitudes toward lepers. His biographers wrote that he actually used to run the other way when he saw a leper coming and would hold his nose to be spared the stench.[11] Given the thirteenth-century view of lepers and St. Francis's genteel disposition before his conversion, it is awesome that he embraced a leper, kissed another, and ate with many others. He even required that his brothers spend time living with lepers as part of their formation.

Why did he do this? Because his experience taught him that embracing and living with lepers was the surest way to God and the quickest way to self-knowledge. St. Francis learned that there was really no difference between the lepers and himself. Certainly he had better clothes, was more educated, and looked nicer. But all of these were only externals that created the illusion that he was different from others. He learned that we are all God's creatures. In embracing lepers, St. Francis accomplished two things. First, he embraced himself. Accepting the leper was accepting himself as he really was. Second, his solidarity with the leper led to the deepest communion with God.

St. Francis's experience was a new model for the spiritual life. For many centuries the Christian spiritual journey was placed in the context of the doctrine of the three ways. The purgative way, which included a turning away from all sin, was the beginning of the spiritual life. Once this was accomplished, one's energy focused on growth in virtue. This was called the illuminative way. The hope was that after a long period of virtuous living, one would reach the unitive way, which was intimate communion with God.

St. Francis's embrace of the leper introduced another way of looking at the doctrine of the three ways. His inner journey led him outside himself to the God who was in rejected people. By going among those who are suffering and poor, the purgation that occurred for him was a shifting of values. The pain of purgation was the rejection by family and friends who lived by the culture's values. He found a new way of looking at the poor and suffering that was countercultural. He no longer saw them as different but rather as brothers and sisters who had much to teach him about God and prayer.

As he experienced lepers as human beings, he no longer treated them as objects. Instead of attempting to practice many virtues, Francis found all virtue in compassion toward lepers. This realization was his enlightenment and illumination.

The more compassionate he was toward the marginated, the more human and holy he became. His solidarity with lepers led to union with God. Although St. Francis did not directly challenge oppressive systems, his life of solidarity with lepers was an indictment on the values of his culture.

Conclusion

Our God writes straight with crooked lines. The God whom we worship does not cause or will suffering. Our God calls us to the fullness of life by embracing with love the pain in our lives and the world around us. Those very situations that are so filled with the evils of pain and suffering can become the occasions for personal growth, deeper compassion for the marginated, and intimate communion with God. As we struggle with shifting social structures in America, God calls us to a new lifestyle, to let go of a class system that excludes people and dehumanizes them. God is to be found in the lepers who walk on Wall Street, live in Harlem, or work on farms in developing countries. Wherever a human being cries out, whether because of emotional or physical pain or deprivation, God is waiting there to be embraced. This is the spiritual journey for the twenty-first century.

REFLECTION STARTERS

1. What are some of the ways you run away from emptiness and pain in your life? What are the questions and issues that you feel? What do you need to do to face them?

2. Who are the lepers that you encounter in your family, parish, school, or world? Can you think of ways of embracing them?

3. How do you feel about the church's shift from its option for the middle class to its option for the poor? What do your actions and attitudes say about where your personal option lies?

4. Reflect on a personal experience of suffering. What were your feelings? Who and where was God in the process? Was it a source of growth? Are there any unresolved religious or personal issues remaining from this experience?

5. Spend some time with the book of Job. How do you identify with Job? His friends? What is your reaction to God's speeches?

CHAPTER FOUR

A Spirituality of Collaboration

The best thing to give your enemy is forgiveness; to an opponent, tolerance; to a friend, your heart; to your child, a good example; to yourself, respect; to all, charity.
— FRANCIS M. BALFOUR

FOCUS QUESTIONS

- What's your definition of love?

- What are you feeling right now? Feel the feeling and describe it in writing.

- Are you a team player or would you rather work alone?

- How can you forgive someone and still feel hurt? What do you do if you find that you just cannot forgive someone?

Building a Cathedral

"With huge sums of money on the line, traders have no time to attend to fallen colleagues," notes the *Wall Street Journal*. When an elderly gentleman had a heart attack on the trading floor as the bell rang, no one stopped to help him because it could have meant the loss of thousands of dollars. The very

89

same week *Forbes* magazine carried an article entitled "Why Aren't We Happy When We Have Everything We Want?" The article depicted the absence of meaning in the lives of many Americans. Part of the reason for this is that we live fragmented lives. We're nice in church, but not in the parking lot. And certainly not on the trading floor. We will fill the void felt by so many to the degree that we can bring charity, compassion, and collaboration into the parking lot and onto the trading floor.

It is easy to lose the larger picture when we are absorbed in the details of daily life. In the Middle Ages, people spent hours arguing about issues such as how many angels could dance on the head of a pin. We laugh at these things today because now we put our worlds together differently. We can have the illusion that we are concerned about the larger issues such as the world economy, nuclear weapons, and ecology while we neglect to take care of the needs of the people in front of us.

The critical issue for all ages is that people be concerned about the real questions and needs of life. A story is told about a cathedral that was being built in France. An inspector went in and asked people what they were doing. The first man he saw said, "I'm making stained-glass windows." The visitor commented on their beauty and walked along to the next person. "I'm making a mosaic. I've been working on this for about six months now. I should be finished by Christmas." He then noticed a wood carver. He said, "What are you carving?" She responded, "I'm making a statue of St. Joseph that will be placed on the side altar shrine." Finally, the inspector went to a little old lady, "And you, what are you doing?" She looked up for a moment and said, "I'm building a cathedral." Then she peacefully went back to her work.

The little old lady saw the bigger picture. Often religious people lose sight of the bigger picture while working in the marketplace. We can become so preoccupied with details and tangents that the essence of the Gospel is often lost. Jesus gave us the perspective of the larger picture: "You shall love the Lord your God with your whole heart, with your whole soul, and with all your mind. This is the greatest and first commandment. The second is like it: You shall love your neighbor as yourself. On these two commandments the whole law is based, and the prophets as well" (Matt. 22:37–38). Charity is what life is all about. St. Paul writes that it is the greatest of all the gifts. To paraphrase his famous letter to the Corinthians, What good is it if we have money, talent, and position? What does it matter if we call ourselves religious and have degrees in theology? What difference does it make if we are the CEO of the largest firm on Wall Street and own the biggest home in town? If we don't have charity, we have nothing at all.

Damn It, Do It!

The early Christians were recognized by their charity: "See how they love one another." Christians were immediately spotted in a crowd because of their love. A story is told of St. John, the great apostle of charity. He constantly went about saying the same three words, "Love one another." Legend has it that these were his dying words.

When I was in the seminary in the late 1960s and early 1970s, the big word was "Love." It was the post–Vatican II era, the height of the Vietnam War, and the time of the trauma of the inner-city riots. People were beginning to realize that traditional religion and the American politics of the 1950s were no longer working. I think that the focus on love was a way of grasping for another way of expressing newly felt religious, social, and political needs. People yearned for a freshness, a newness that love might bring. The banners, books, and songs all carried this theme.

People naively thought that they were discovering love for the first time. What sometimes followed was a shallow, trendy, and rootless expression of love. The sexual revolution thrived in this milieu. "Love and do what you will" became the order of the day. Outmoded rules and taboos were abandoned and a new freedom summoned people to love.

The problem with this fascination with love is that the deepest meaning of the word was lost. Love became like the Latin word *res*. This word means "thing." If you were to look up this word in a Latin dictionary, there would be over a hundred possible meanings for the word. The result is that it is almost impossible to translate the word accurately. Look up the word "love" in Webster and you'll have the same experience. The list of definitions includes affection for another, attractions based on sexual desire, affection based on admiration, warmth, copulation, and unselfish loyal and benevolent concern for the good of another.

The confusion lies in the fact that the word "love" has absorbed the definitions of "lust," "desire," and "sexual" appetite. When the word love is used in a song or a poem, it is hard to distinguish the actual meaning. Thus, the power of the classical meaning of the word has been lost in our culture. Many people are in love with a false idea of love. At its best and purest form, love means sacrifice, care, unselfishness, giving, understanding, and generosity with no strings attached.

An old priest friend of mine used to say, "When all is said and done, more is said than done." And so it's been with love. The story is told of a suburban parish that voted to reflect on the theme of love for the four Sundays of Advent. Banners were made for each week. The first week the altar server carried the banner in the procession that read, "Love one another as I have loved you." The second week's banner read, "Be a little more careful of love." The banner for the third week summoned the congregation to "Rejoice in love." Finally, a little old man walked down the aisle on the fourth Sunday of Advent with his banner, "Damn it, do it."

All of this came home to me when my friend, Mary Ellen, was dying of cancer. While she was still well enough, she had a dinner party for her closest friends. She wanted to spend time with us. She put together a beautiful prayer service in which she thanked God for each of us. She then shared stories of an intimate or enjoyable time she had with each person. We laughed and cried. At the end of the service she gave us special farewell gifts. I treasure the plaque she gave me with the famous line from *Les Miserables*, "To love another person is to see the face of God."

Mary Ellen went out in style. For many reasons she was a precious gift to me because she taught me the true meaning of life and love. When she died, I said, "Damn it, do it!" We're only here for a short time, and the most important thing we can do wherever we spend our days, even if on the trading floor, is to live Christ's most important teaching: "Love one another, even as I have loved you."

Love from the Neck Up

The Song of Songs begins with the words, "More delightful is your love than wine!" (Song 1:2). If you take a few minutes to read through the Song of Songs, you will find a love poem that is filled with feelings. Love is not just an intellectual concept, lived from the neck up. It includes feelings and some of these feelings can be quite passionate. I choose the Song of Songs as an example because it has occasioned much controversy over the centuries. Commentaries about this work have been written by such great masters as Origen, Gregory of Nyssa, Bernard of Clairvaux, and John of the Cross. Many of these writers categorized the Song of Songs as an allegory about God's love and the call to live in union with God.[1]

That is not the only way to view this piece of writing. It can also be looked at from a literal point of view. This is where the debates have come in over the years. The high level of feelings in the Song of Songs gave scandal to many of the Jewish rabbis. As late as the second century, they still did not agree that the book should be included in the sacred canon. Christians continued to elaborate on the allegory track, asserting that the love of the bridegroom for the bride was a symbol of Christ's love for the church.

In the later part of the nineteenth century, scholars discovered close parallels between the language of the Song of Songs and Arab wedding songs from Syria. These wedding customs included a dance with a sword by the bride on the day prior to the wedding in which she described her own beauty ("I am as dark, but lovely as the tents of Kedar," Song 1:5; "I am a flower of Sharon, a lily of the valley," 2:1). For a week after the wedding, the couple was treated as a king and queen with festive parties and songs extolling the couple's beauty ("My lover's body is a work of ivory covered with sapphires. His stature is like the trees of Lebanon," 5:14). The religious use of such love songs may even go back to hymns and ceremonies surrounding the sacred marriage rituals of the Canaanite followers of Baal. There is no doubt that the content of the Song of Songs includes the component of human emotions.

To be human is to have emotions. Feelings are integral to love. While it is true that love is a decision and not a feeling, feelings add zest and passion to any relationship. A relationship that has no feelings is in trouble.

The long debates about the Song of Songs over the centuries reveal a deep-rooted suspicion of feelings. It is true that to seek feelings alone can be narcissistic and negate the possibility of long-term relationships. To be in a relationship only to fulfill a commitment is to live life from the neck up. Commitment, decision, and feelings make relationships come alive because these ingredients integrate body, soul, and spirit.

Education from the Neck Down

In addition to being an allegory about Christ's love for the church, the Song of Songs also teaches a spirituality of feelings. In this poetic piece, two people experience the beauty and power of feelings and creatively and constructively articulate these emotions to enhance their relationship. The Song of Songs demonstrates how feelings can draw us closer to God and one another. It's a matter of choice. When we know what we feel we can choose to express ourselves in ways that are life-giving. Not to know what we feel can mean that we will be driven by our feelings. This can be very destructive. Dealing with feelings is a powerful way of being holy in the midst of everyday life. Often what makes daily life so sterile is that feelings are not freely exchanged.

In the movie *Ryan's Daughter,* a disappointed wife goes to her minister to complain about her marriage. He responds by telling her that her husband is a good provider and caretaker of the home. She responded, "Yes, I know. But he lacks passion." He was living up to his part of the marriage contract. He provided a beautifully structured house but did not bring the passion that would make it into a home.

The notion of commitment needs to be accompanied by some kind of tangible expression of love. A friend told me that her high school graduating class had just had their twenty-fifth reunion. She was part of the planning committee. The class refused to invite their principal to the reunion. Twenty-five years later they were still furious with him. My friend told me that the tragedy was that the principal did all the right things. He ran the best school in the city, but he did it mechanically and without any feeling. It was impossible for the students, even twenty-five years later, to see that there was love beneath the principal's severity. I know the principal. He is a dedicated man. The flaw is that he assumed that the students would one day appreciate that his unrelenting strictness was an expression of care and concern.

To live without knowing our feelings and how to express them is sad. "Feelings 101" teaches that we need to listen to our feelings and spend time with them. Get to know your feelings. Do not be afraid of them. Feelings are neither good nor bad in themselves. They just are. What we do with our feelings is another question. It is not always appropriate or wise to act on feelings. Conversely, it is astute to trust that your feelings reveal something about yourself. Try to never be afraid of the intensity of your feelings. How feelings are experienced will vary for each individual. What does not vary is that feelings run deep. To be truly aware is to be in touch with the intensity of what we feel.

A way that I deal with feelings is to let them just be. I try not to fight feelings or make believe that I don't have them. I do this is several ways. I let my feelings happen in prayer. I let them be and talk to the Lord about them. If I am having trouble getting in touch with a feeling, I will then begin to write about it in my journal. I'll give it a color, a name, and even an odor. I'll trace when and why I first experienced the feeling. This has often helped me to know what's going on here and now. Let me give two examples.

What to Do with Sexual Feelings? When I was in the seminary, most of my feelings were repressed. We lived in an environment where we just did not talk about what we were feeling. Many of my sexual feelings were ignored during that whole time.

When I was first ordained and was assigned to a parish, it took me a long time to become comfortable in interacting with women. When I began to ask myself why, I realized that I was afraid of sexual feelings. This all came to a head when I noticed sexual feelings toward a woman who worked closely with me on several parish council committees. It was hard for me to face these feelings, but I forced myself. When I brought them to my prayer, I noticed the intensity of the feeling and I just let it be. I then asked the Lord to come and be with me in the feeling. After the prayer I thought for a few days about the various options I had in dealing with the feelings. I decided that I wanted to keep my celibate commitment and at the same time have a close friendship with this woman.

After getting a further handle on the situation by talking it through with a counselor, I decided to talk to the woman about it since I knew that she had similar feelings toward me. I was aware of the risk of the sexual attraction that could occur in having this conversation. In being honest about the feelings and talking about them openly, I found that they were now life-sized and manageable. We made a decision together to have a close friendship but a nongenital one. What I found in this experience was that I could make a decision about what I would do with my feelings. I am still very close to this woman. We have a healthy relationship, one that I believe has made me much more human and closer to God.[2]

What to Do with Anger? Another feeling that I never learned how to deal with in the seminary was anger. What I did learn was how to bury anger. Anger is always a secondary emotion. There is generally an underlying issue or event that brings about the anger. Sometimes this can be so deeply rooted that getting to its core is like peeling layers off an onion. Just keep remembering that the hard work of introspection is worth it. Consider the alternative. Negative expressions of anger can be very ugly, e.g., hostility, passive aggression, addictions (to alcohol, work, drugs, eating, etc.), headaches, backaches, and stomach disorders.

I grew up thinking that it was a sin to feel angry. Whenever I felt angry, my initial reaction was to feel guilty for the feeling. It was one of my usual listings of sins for confession: "Father, forgive me. I was angry." It took a long time to learn that anger is permissible. In fact, it is an ordinary component of being human.

Eventually, I allowed myself the freedom to feel the anger. Just as with sexual feelings, I was then capable of making choices about my anger rather than allowing myself to be led by it.

I learned about unresolved anger the hard way. I lived in a house with a very troubled confrere. No local community wanted him. There was no place for him to go. I became the target of all his anger. He was mean and nasty. He did everything he could to undermine everything I was trying to do. I was literally beside myself, blaming myself, feeling angry at him, and living in fear of what he was going to do next. I even went so far as to lock my doors when he was home.

I was very honest and open with the local superior at staff meetings. He appeared totally sympathetic and in agreement with me. He would even advise me on concrete actions that I should take in dealing with this priest. It came as a shock to gradually realize that the superior was playing both ends against the middle. It took me a long time to realize that my real anger was at the superior for his duplicity and at other authority figures for not helping me in my pain. I sat and prayed and talked about my anger for a long time. It hurt a lot. Through this process, I understood that the hostile priest was a sick man who could not help himself. I came to realize that my real disappointment was that my brothers were not there to help me. I suddenly knew that the feeling underneath the anger was the deep hurt of abandonment and disappointment in the failure of people to meet my expectations. It took me a lot of praying, spiritual direction, and some therapy to work through all of this. If I ran from the feelings and the pain, I probably would be a very bitter man today. Dealing with the feelings and letting go of expectations finally led to forgiveness and inner peace. It all came down to facing feelings and making choices. My experience has been that truly dealing with feelings frees us from fear, repression, and depression and leads to a life that is human and happy.[3]

A Marriage Almost Destroyed by Pistachio Nuts

Once we know our feelings, then we have to learn to express them. Dostoyevsky wrote that "much unhappiness has come into the world because of bewilderment and things left unsaid."[4] If we really care about one another, we need to articulate our feelings. In doing this, we are telling one another who we are. It is unfortunate that people often are left wondering what's going on because we don't speak from our hearts.

Communication is the key to any good relationship. Conversation that is concerned only about ideas can be interesting but it rarely creates intimacy. The communication of feelings, especially hard feelings, can lead to real union. Withholding these feelings can even be destructive. The key to the union of hearts experienced in the Song of Songs was that the bride and groom communicated their feelings to one another. Throughout the entire piece the couple is constantly telling one another how much they miss one another, how beautiful they are, and how deeply they care for each other. This kind of communication is thoroughly challenging.

I'll give you a bizarre but true example of what the lack

of communication can cause. One weekend my sister, Pauline, went on a shopping tour with some of her friends. When she returned home, she noticed that there were cigarettes with lipstick stains in the ash tray. Instead of being direct in her communication with my brother-in-law, Lou, she said, "Did anyone stop by to visit while I was away?" He said, "No." She stretched her inquiry further: "What did you do all weekend?" He answered, "I was out most of the time. It was kind of boring. I didn't do that much. I missed you."

Pauline was furious. She assumed that he was lying. She wouldn't talk to him for a week and never confronted him about the cigarette butts. Instead of expressing her feelings of anger and disappointment, she bottled them up. Eventually, they came to a truce and at least began talking to each other again. They weren't close because they were not communicating their real feelings and a little wall had grown up between them. A low level of tension continued.

One night Lou was watching TV while smoking Salem cigarettes and eating pistachio nuts. Suddenly, Pauline noticed that the pistachio nuts were leaving a red smudge (like lipstick!) on the filters. She cried out, "Oh, my God, it wasn't another woman after all. It was the pistachio nuts!" When she finally told Lou what was bothering her, he said, "Why didn't you tell me this was what was on your mind? I haven't been able to figure you out for a week and have felt very confused and distant." The moral of the story is that the choice to communicate your feelings is a critical one that can lead either to closeness or to distance. Communication of feelings is key to relationships. Don't let pistachio nuts destroy your relationships.

Collaborate or Die

Pauline and Lou are not the first nor the last to argue about relationships. In fact, another argument on the same theme took place back in the thirteenth century between St. Thomas Aquinas and St. Bonaventure. They began with a friendly discussion on their worldviews. The discussion became quite heated and degenerated into an argument.

Thomas said, "The world can be defined by causality. Everything is cause and effect." When Bonaventure asked him what he meant by this, Thomas responded, "It is quite simple. God is the Prime Mover. He created the world and causes it to continue to exist." St. Thomas developed his whole system of proofs for God's existence based on his foundation of cause and effect.

St. Bonaventure was troubled by Thomas's approach. He thought long and hard and concluded that there was another way of seeing reality. He reflected on his own experience and wrote that the Trinity is the key. He said to Aquinas, "The relationships between Father, Son, and Holy Spirit are the essence of reality." From this network of relationships, St. Bonaventure saw all creation as connected and as mirroring the Trinity. He carried all of this to its logical conclusion and said, "I would even go so far as to say that we exist only insofar as we are in relationship to God and one another. If we are not living this network of relationships, then we do not even exist."[5]

Strong words. Maybe even scary. Contemporary American culture would have a lot of trouble with St. Bonaventure. Individualism is a dominant characteristic of our culture. Alexis de Tocqueville, the French social philosopher, in his book *Democracy in America,* written in the 1830s, noted many strong aspects of the American character that would build a great nation and contribute to the world community. At the same time, he warned that our tendency toward individualism could eventually isolate Americans and undermine the conditions of freedom.[6]

I believe that collectively facing and expressing our feelings will strengthen our country, churches, and families. If we can learn to express our love for one another and to deal with our anger and frustrations with one another, it will certainly be a step in the right direction in building a better world. Honestly expressing our feelings gives hope that issues can be resolved and plans can be made for a better future. This collective process is called collaboration.

Given the critical circumstances of the twentieth century, I would take St. Bonaventure's bold statement and make it even bolder. If we do not learn how to collaborate, we will die. The world must collaborate if the economy is to be sound and the problems of ecology are to be resolved. Americans need to collaborate to deal with the problems of crime and drug abuse. Religions must collaborate and make friends with each other if our message about the Golden Rule is to be credible. In light of today's issues, I think it is now immoral to do anything alone that can be done with others.

I remember visiting religious houses in Europe in the 1980s. Many of these houses were international communities serving its worldwide members. On several occasions, I was shocked to discover that nationalism was sometimes stronger among members than their religious bonds. Each country has its own narrow agenda and turf to protect. If the world is to survive, these divisions must be dissolved.

Competition and parochialism among church people is scandalous. Interacting with programs, personnel, and finances among churches should be the rule, not the exception. Collaboration should even cross denominational lines. Americans need to look beyond the narrow and somewhat artificial political party lines to the larger good and needs of the country. The world community needs to see the relationships between countries, especially when it comes to sharing resources. We will exist to the degree that we are willing to learn how to collaborate.

It is a difficult skill to learn. Several years ago, I was on a committee to establish a collaborative formation program in the United States. It was a challenge to get beyond prejudices, turf protection, and hidden agendas. My experience was that as relationships began to develop and walls came down, people gradually began to care and trust one another. Collaboration began to happen to the degree that we were honest with our feelings and loving in our expression of them to one another.

The Song of Collaboration

I think that there is no better poetic expression of the spirituality of collaboration than in the *Canticle of Brother Sun*. This song written by St. Francis of Assisi is a summary of all that he believed about life. The *Canticle* is about the connections St. Francis experienced in the universe.

This is the song for the mystic in the marketplace. The song fixes life's goals on God and weaves the connections among all created things. St. Francis and his friars sang this song in Assisi's marketplace, calling people to higher values. In the same spirit of the Song of Songs, this is a magnificent expression of feelings. This poetic piece is an expression St. Francis's love for the beauty of the universe and the God who created it. Here is a magnificent example of someone who is totally free in expressing what was felt most deeply within his heart.

The Poor Man of Assisi began writing this piece in 1224 and completed it just before he died in 1226. I invite you now to spend a few minutes praying and reflecting on these words.

Most high, almighty, wonderful Lord.
   To you belongs praise, glory, honor and every blessing.

These belong only to you, Most High God,
and no one is worthy even to say your name.

Be praised, my Lord, with all your creatures,
   especially Sir Brother Sun,
who is the day, and through him you shed light upon us.

And he is beautiful and radiant with great splendor,
and he resembles you, Most High God.

Be praised, my Lord, through Sister Moon and Stars,
you formed them in the heavens bright, and precious, and
   beautiful.

Be praised, my Lord, through Brother Wind
and through the air, cloudy and serene, and every kind of
   weather,
through which you nourish all creation.

Be praised, my Lord, through Sister Water,
who is very useful and humble and precious and pure.

Be praised, my Lord, through Brother Fire,
by whom you illumine the night;
he is beautiful, playful, vigorous, and strong.

Be praised, my Lord, through our Sister Mother Earth,
who sustains and guides us,
and produces a variety of fruits, along with colored flowers and herbs.

Be praised, my Lord, through those who forgive for love
of you,
and who bear sickness and trials.

Happy are those who persevere in peace,
for by you, Most High God, they shall be rewarded.

Be praised, my Lord, through our Sister Bodily Death,
whom no living person is able to avoid.

Woe to those who die in mortal sin.
Happy are they whom death will find faithful to your holy
will,
for the second death shall do them no harm.

Praise and bless my Lord
and serve God with thanksgiving and great humility.[7]

This prayer is truly upbeat and beautiful. What is not in any
way obvious is that St. Francis was anything but upbeat and
beautiful when he wrote this piece. This poem, which extols
the splendor of nature, was written when St. Francis was in a
state of deep depression and was suffering from a painful eye
ailment. His eyes had to be covered during the day because they
could not bear the sunlight. He could no longer look at the sun
he loved so dearly. His words were written in physical darkness
and emotional despair.

The Sun, Moon, and Wind are symbols for the Father, Son,
and Spirit. St. Francis's vision is one of a connected universe

that reflects the unity of the Trinity. The names of the elements are prefaced with the familial terms of "brother," "sister," and "mother," highlighting the care and tenderness with which all creation must be treated. St. Francis praises those who offer pardon because they restore harmony and a peaceful rhythm to the universe. The key to the whole canticle is the virtues of gratitude and humility. "Give him thanks and serve him with humility" was originally the refrain sung after each verse of the canticle. It is the grateful and humble heart that knows feelings of both love and hurt and makes choices to reach out to create relationships in the midst of a broken world.

I would like to rename St. Francis's prayer. I'll call it *The Song of Collaboration*. This could be the prayer said at every United Nations meeting, ecumenical service, and political rally. If all would join hands in an act of solidarity, then we would have a future filled with hope. The choice is ours: sing and dance a new song created from collaboration or recite the death chant occasioned by indifference and individualism.

Forget the Textbooks

Collaboration invites us to treat people with respect and equality. It would be wonderful if religious denominations could lead the way in modeling collaboration. Too often the worst kind of discrimination is religious exclusion. It is especially sad to see the many divisions within Christianity. Religion can lead the way to collaboration by genuinely entering into interreligious dialogue. No one has a monopoly on the truth or a corner on the market in its understanding of God. We need to pool our experiences and traditions to begin to paint a composite picture of God.

Religious people are supposed to be concerned about the most profound issues, yet often they are absorbed with the most trivial. Many cruel and cutting things have been done in the name of God. Be careful of people who speak for God rather than speaking with God. Events like the Inquisition illustrate the judgmental and harsh attitudes that can infiltrate even the religious psyche.

I remember as a young boy being taught that "there was no salvation outside the church." We were also told to avoid Protestants because they were our enemies. We lived in an Italian Catholic neighborhood. Imagine the raised eyebrows in the early 1950s when Protestants moved into the neighborhood. I became friends with Andrew, a young Protestant boy my age. I remember not being able to sleep at night because I thought that Andrew would not be coming to heaven with the rest of us Catholic children. I liked him and wanted him to come with us. With that agenda, a few of us took our Baltimore catechisms in hand and went over and tried to convert Andrew.

A few years later, Andrew's sister, Meg, was marrying my Catholic cousin. The marriage was to take place outside a Catholic church. I still remember the lengthy discussions and arguments in the neighborhood, "Should we go to the wedding?" "Should we bring gifts because that signifies approval?"

I discovered years later that in that same era Cardinal Cushing was making one of his periodic visits to the major seminary. He told the seminarians, "The textbooks will tell you not to associate with Protestants. Okay," he said, "write that down on the examination papers to keep the professors happy." Then he added, "When you are ordained, forget the textbooks. Be friends with Protestants. You'll find that they are just as good if not better than we are. Be kind and welcoming to all people."

Fortunately, Cardinal Cushing's approach gained momentum. In the late 1950s, at the height of the cold war, Nikita Khrushchev's son-in-law announced that he was to visit the Vatican. The eyes of the world were upon Pope John XXIII to see what he was going to do when this atheistic communist came to St. Peter's.

It was a beautiful sight. The pope wobbled down the hallway to meet and embrace the man, a scene reminiscent of the parable of the Prodigal Son. As he was leaving, the pope embraced him again and said, "Do you mind if this old man gives you a blessing for your children?" John XXIII taught us a powerful lesson that day. His approach to Khrushchev's son-in-law was loving and invitational. His reference to himself as an old man was totally nonthreatening. Who could not love a jolly old man? His request to send a blessing to the children was thoughtful and sensitive. Who doesn't want the very best for their children? John XXIII was truly a mystic in the world who opened his arms and heart to everyone. These are the attitudes that are needed to make collaboration happen and to shatter individualism.

Name Your God

The way we look at God will influence all our attitudes. If our God is harsh and judgmental, we will act accordingly. These attitudes certainly do not foster collaboration. On the other hand, a loving and forgiving God opens us up to all kinds of people and viewpoints.

This is illustrated by the way some people connect God with the AIDS virus. The virus is causing a physical and spiritual crisis in our world. Underneath the symptoms of AIDS lurk many serious psychological and theological issues. Emotional healing needs to take place in individuals and families affected by HIV. Spiritual healing is needed in the perception that many have of God's role in this disease.

Some fundamentalists would reject the sin and the sinner. They would make outcasts of people suffering with HIV. The theological underpinning of their social stance is that God causes AIDS as a punishment for sin. They image God as being angry and vindictive. He is a God who is waiting for creatures to make that one wrong move so that they can be sentenced to eternal damnation. I grew up with this kind of God image.

When I was in the third grade, a group of friends came and asked me if I would like to join them in cutting down a tree. I thought that this was a wonderful idea. We looked for the biggest tree in an empty lot. It was about forty feet tall. We chopped, axed, and sawed. To us little guys, it seemed like we were knocking down the World Trade Center. It was an exhilarating feeling.

As we were savoring the feeling, some budding moral theologian in the group suggested that we had just committed a mortal sin. When he made the announcement, our first reaction was "Thank God it is Saturday. We can go to confession before we get hit by lightning and all wind up in hell." We suddenly felt like criminals, laden with guilt for the crime that we had just committed.

All fifteen of us traipsed off to confession. I began with the usual, "Bless me, Father, for I have sinned." Then I confessed our offense. "I cut down a tree." The priest then asked me, "Was this tree dead or alive?" "It was alive, Father." He told me that this was pretty serious and that for a penance I should say a rosary.

After all of us had confessed, we met outside church. When we compared notes on what had happened, we discovered that the priest had asked all of us the same questions. Some in the group told him that the tree was alive and others said that it was dead. Those of us in the alive group convinced the dead group that they had just committed another mortal sin. Off they went back into the confessional to confess their new mortal sin. They told the priest, "Father, we told you the tree was dead. It wasn't dead, it was alive, but now it is dead."

The same kind of God that would punish people with AIDS is the kind of God who would send little boys to hell for all eternity for chopping down a tree. It's the God that parents in days gone by used to bring law and order into the household. "Don't do that, God is going to punish you." Whenever my mother would make pizza, she would warn us, "If you take a slice before dinner, God will be very angry at you." Not only does God not care if I were to take a slice before dinner, but probably would say, "Eat the whole pie. Enjoy."

The image of the God who is anger-filled and waiting for the opportunity to inflict pain and punishment needs to be corrected. This is certainly not the way God is described in the

Hebrew and Christian Scriptures. The God of Israel is a God who totally favors the people. This God is like the good parent who wants only what is best for the children's happiness and well-being. In the Christian Scripture, Jesus tells us to call our God "Abba" or "Daddy." It is eminently clear that God is always ready to forgive us and loves us beyond telling. Read Luke 15, the story of the prodigal son, also referred to as the parable of the forgiving father. It is a magnificent story. After reading the story and the image of God portrayed there, I challenge anyone to demonstrate that our God is a cruel, angry, punishing God.

Jonathan helped me to reimage God in my life. I taught Jonathan in the ninth grade. After not seeing him for twenty years, he called me several weeks before Christmas to tell me he had AIDS. I visited him on Christmas morning. Before his death several months later, I grew very close to him. The time I spent with him was grace-filled.

One day while visiting him, he said to me, "I have clothes in my closet that I know that I will never be well enough to wear again. Please take them and give them to the poor." I tearfully emptied his closet and brought his beautiful clothes to the poor. This was a blessed moment for me. In his suffering, Jonathan was more concerned about the pain of others. I experienced this same spirit in him many times. For example, on another occasion, he said to me, "Please help me to plan my funeral." I told him what a privilege this would be for me. He told me, "I want to do this in order to make things easier for my parents and family."

My final visit with Jonathan before he died was on Holy Thursday. On that day, he wanted to review his life with me, receive the sacrament of reconciliation, and prepare to meet God. His confession was one of the most beautiful I've experienced. He had truly learned the lessons of life. Jonathan learned that God loved him unconditionally and that love spilled over into the compassion that characterized his life.

On that last day I was with Jonathan, I prayed with him a prayer that images God the way I have come to know God:

KNOWN

I know you. I created you. I am creating you. I have loved you from your mother's womb. You have fled — as you now know — from my love. But I love you nevertheless and not-the-less and, however far you flee, it is I who sustain your very power of fleeing, and I will never let you go. I accept you as you are. You are forgiven. I know all your sufferings. I have always known them. For beyond your understanding, when you suffer, I suffer. I also know all of the little tricks by which you try to hide the ugliness you have made of your life from yourself and others. But you are beautiful. You are beautiful more deeply within than you can see. You are beautiful because you yourself, in the unique one that only you are, reflect already something of the beauty of my holiness in a way which never ends. You are beautiful also because I, and I alone, see the beauty you shall become. Through the transforming power of my love you shall become perfectly beautiful in a uniquely irreplaceable way, which neither you nor I will work out alone. For we shall work it out together.[8]

Seventy Times Seven

The final obstacle to collaboration is the inability to forgive. Emotional health is essential to physical and spiritual well-being. The key to emotional vitality is forgiveness. It is only when we accept God's forgiveness that we can begin to forgive ourselves and others. The False Self would resist God's forgiveness, telling us that we are unworthy of God's mercy. Its purpose is to keep us in a state of guilt. We need to learn to say "No" to the voice of the False Self and "Yes" to the voice of the Holy Spirit, who tells us that we are good and all is forgivable.

Boundless charity is the willingness and ability to offer forgiveness to all people, especially those who have hurt us most deeply. It is impossible to do this unless we have first forgiven ourselves. Jesus' message on the cross was that all is forgivable and that everything is correctable. He prayed, "Father, forgive them. They know not what they do." Jesus taught us how to put charity in action by a constant willingness to forgive others.

My favorite person in the New Testament is the good thief. Tradition has named him Dismas. Here is a thief, someone who probably committed every sin in the book. Interesting that he is the only person in the New Testament that we can say with certainty is in heaven. Christ's words to him, "Today you will be with me in paradise" (Luke 23:43), echo through the centuries, challenging people to live charity through forgiveness.

Jesus' message to St. Peter that he must be ready to forgive seventy times seven was really shocking news (Matt. 18:22). The law of talion required that one be ready to forgive several times within a lifetime. Jesus' seventy times seven is the Hebrew equivalent for eternity. The teaching is that the way to peace is endless forgiveness. There is great psychological wisdom in the Gospel mandate to leave your gifts at the altar and first go be reconciled and then come back. The axiom is simple: if you are not at peace with the people in your life, then you cannot be at peace with God.

"Turn the other cheek" is to be taken literally. In forgiving my brothers and sisters, I am actually forgiving myself. If the person who strikes me is unforgivable, then so am I. It is an all-or-nothing proposition: Everything is forgivable or nothing is. To offer forgiveness to others is to have accepted forgiveness in my life. Perhaps Gandhi is the best contemporary example of a person who was so at peace within himself and so accepting of God's forgiveness that he had the freedom to offer peaceful nonresistance to the evil he encountered in others.

You might say, "All of this is pie in the sky." In a way, it is. Just thinking about forgiveness or even agreeing with the principles written here does not mean that forgiveness is manifested in my life. I want to propose some practical principles for the implementation of Jesus' teaching.

- *Principle One:* ACCEPT THAT IT'S OKAY TO BE HURT
  Remember, feelings are neutral. If someone has hurt you,

it is important to begin by saying: "I feel hurt." Pretending that you are not hurt, or that you can offer instant forgiveness, can cause more harm than good. Denial can be destructive to yourself. It can also do more harm to the person who offended you because your hurt might be expressed in subtle, inappropriate, confusing ways.

- *Principle Two:* TRY TO UNDERSTAND WHY YOU ARE HURT
  Getting to the root will help you realize what it is within yourself that makes it hard for you to forgive. Root causes can be anything: Was this a blow to your pride? Did it remind you of a past unresolved hurt? Were you treated without respect and dignity?

- *Principle Three:* CHANGE WHAT YOU CAN CHANGE
  Change the areas in your life that you are able to change. In dealing with your issues, you will come to a deeper integration. This will better enable you to offer peace to the person who offended you.

- *Principle Four:* WALK IN THEIR MOCCASINS
  There is a familiar Indian proverb: "Do not criticize others until you have walked a mile in their moccasins." Get into their skin. Why did they do what they did? Did they deliberately set out to hurt you? Was their action simply an expression of their own brokenness or a cry for help or attention? Frequently people who hurt others are projecting their own brokenness onto others.

- *Principle Five:* CHANGE YOUR PERCEPTION
  If you are able to see the other as a brother or sister who is acting out of hurt and if you are able to offer your hand in forgiveness, then do so.

- *Principle Six:* REMEMBER THAT FORGIVENESS IS A PROCESS
  If you are unable to offer forgiveness right away, that is all right. You cannot be who you are not. What you can do is begin the process. Pray for the grace to forgive. If your heart does not begin to soften after a few weeks, then find someone to talk to like a friend, clergyperson, counselor,

or therapist. It does not matter how long it takes. What matters is that you keep on trying.

Forgiveness heals relationships and is the most profound expression of charity. The inability to forgive stifles and destroys relationships, while pardoning the faults and shortcomings of others opens the door to collaboration. Although forgiveness is a difficult process for most of us, the alternative is far worse. The experience of forgiveness is truly a grace: "The ineffable joy of forgiving and being forgiven forms an ecstasy that might well arouse the envy of the gods."[9]

Conclusion

As we live everyday life, it is important that we not forget what life really is. Feeling our feelings and expressing them gives vitality to our relationships and our world. Collaboration is a strong vehicle for expressing the essence of charity in a practical way. Collaboration rests on a positive notion of God and an ever-ready willingness to forgive our neighbor so that we will always be ready to forge new and creative relationships, individually and collectively. Like St. Francis in his canticle, we will give praise to God to the degree that we are instruments in collaboratively reflecting God's goodness in the universe.

I once heard a story of a nurse who worked in a mental hospital. There was a wing on the top floor where the most difficult patients were kept. One patient was considered absolutely hopeless. Her food was placed on a tray and slipped through her doorway. It was too dangerous to go into the room. The nurse was a deeply sensitive woman. She got the room key one day and went to visit the incurable patient. When she entered, she walked over to the woman and said, "Is there anything I can do for you?" The patient slapped the nurse across the face. She backed off to the other side of the room, hesitated for a minute, and said, "Is there anything else I can do for you?"

As difficult as such an approach might seem, it is the goal of the Christian life. It is charity in action and comes from the depths of a person who knows what she's feeling and why. She knows that her God is a God of love and is able to communicate this truth. This is the attitude that invites collaboration. It takes a deep self-acceptance, an awareness of God's forgiveness, and a compassionate heart to reach out to the world, especially the hurt, alienated, and marginated and to keep on saying, "Is there anything else I can do for you?"

Reflection Starters

1. Spend some time getting in touch with something or someone that angers you. Describe your anger. What does it sound like? Look like? Smell like? What color is it? What is it like for you to be angry? Spend some time thinking and praying about dealing with your anger positively and creatively.

2. Spend some time allowing a sexual fantasy to unfold. What does it tell you about your sexuality? What do you need to do to channel that fantasy into an action that will be open to a real relationship and make you a more loving and caring person? Does the fantasy tell you anything about areas of unfreedom for which you might need healing?

3. What are the things in your life that prevent you from being more collaborative? Are there areas of narrowness, prejudice, or fear that are sentencing you to a narrow individualism?

4. Make a list of the people with whom you are not at peace. Choose one relationship that has the potential of being resolved and use the method proposed in this chapter to move toward forgiveness.

5. Spend some time reading the Song of Songs. Write down all the feelings that you notice. Express your feelings on paper toward someone you love. Find a way with which you are comfortable in expressing these sentiments to the person.

CHAPTER FIVE

Cunning as Serpents, Gentle as Doves

Behold, I am sending you like sheep in the midst of wolves; so be as cunning as serpents and gentle as doves.
— MATTHEW 10:16

FOCUS QUESTIONS

- How is it possible to be like a serpent and a dove at the same time?

- How much of your life is characterized by stress? Do you do anything to alleviate your stress?

- Does being peaceful mean that you shouldn't feel any tension?

- Who should be made anxious by Christ's teachings in the beatitudes and why?

Wolves Becoming Lambs

"Love one another; live collaboratively; forgive one another; share all things in common; turn the other cheek." Are all of these aspirations unrealistic? Is it possible to live these values in the context of an aggressive Western culture? Many people think that love, sharing, and forgiveness place the Christian at a definite disadvantage in the marketplace.

A classmate confirmed this accusation. Recently he was reflecting on our spiritual formation. "They certainly taught us about being as gentle as doves," he said, " but they forgot to include the cunning as serpents part." Many people worship like doves on Sunday, but act like snakes in the marketplace. I think what Matthew is implying in his equation is that life cannot be compartmentalized. The kingdom does not belong to doves or serpents, but to those who can integrate the two. The challenge is in merging apparent opposites. Isaiah had a good insight into this blending:

> Then the wolf shall be a guest of the lamb,
> and the leopard shall lie down with the kid;
> The calf and the young lion shall browse together,
> with a little child to guide them.
> The cow and the bear shall be neighbors,
> together their young shall rest;
> the lion shall eat hay like the ox.
> The baby shall play by the cobra's den,
> and the child lay his hand on the adder's lair.
>
> (Isa. 11:6–8)

Most people seem to think that the wolf shall become like the lamb and the lion like the ox. There is another way of looking at this situation. It is possible that opposites can come together, maintain their distinctiveness, and live in harmony.

The Coincidence of Opposites

The joining together of opposite characteristics is deeply rooted in the human tradition. Primitive myths are filled with such unions as the marriage of the Sky God and Mother Earth. Gods were often portrayed as simultaneously combining harsh and gentle qualities. Taoists portray the fusion of seeming contradictions, such as dark and light, weak and strong, male and female.

The Greeks perceived a cosmic struggle between love and hate, justice and injustice. Heraclitus taught that all opposites were joined together into a god who was said to be day and night, winter and summer, war and peace.

Nicholas of Cusa, a fifteenth-century mystic, channeled this tradition into a framework that he called the "Coincidence of Opposites." He taught that all creation is centered in God, who brings together diversity within harmony. The model par excellence is Christ, who concurrently mirrors humanity and divinity. Nicholas images this vision in his work *The Vision of God,* where he likens God's presence to eyes in a picture. These special eyes see everything simultaneously. They do this without ever moving. The implication is that the diversity of the universe centers and harmonizes in God.[1]

There are several ways of viewing the doctrine of the coincidence of opposites. The first option is a monistic view that absorbs all differences. From this vantage point, opposites cease to exist and are melded into one solid whole. For example, Sankara, the medieval Indian theologian, taught the doctrine of "nondifferentiation." He instructed that the phenomena of the material world is absorbed in the unity of Brahman, which is the only thing that truly exists.

The second possibility is that differences remain, but without any real unity. In fact, there remains a tension among differences. An example is found in ancient Zoroastrianism, in which the principles of good and evil war against each other. This dualism infiltrated Christianity through both Gnosticism and Manichaeism, which held that the spirit is superior to the material world.

The final scenario is one in which opposites come together and continue to exist as opposites. The very union does not abrogate the differences but rather accentuates them. There is even a complementarity that opposites experience in one another. The female and male principles of Taoism and the complementarity of Yin-Yang are illustrations of this approach. It is in this way that opposites can converge without losing their individuality. The lion remains a lion, the lamb stays a lamb, and both live peacefully because differences are centered in God. Basically, it is a respect for God's creation as we find it and not as we think it should be. There is a wisdom in leaving things the way God created them. In this instance, the cunning of the serpent coupled with the gentleness of the dove creates a powerful dynamism that could transform everyday life.[2]

Respond instead of Reacting

The vision of the coincidence of opposites can be helpful for today's fragmented world. Our religious history is one in which we frequently have reacted to situations rather than responding. Because the church at times has associated itself with political and economic power bases, we sometimes have found it difficult to let go of the status quo because we experience a security there.[3] Today it is becoming increasingly difficult to keep up with all the economic, religious, political, and social changes that are going on around us. Western civilization is collapsing. A new world order is about to emerge. This is already happening. We are no longer a bipolar world dominated by two superpowers, the United States and Russia. It is certain that the not too distant future will bring us four or five new superpowers. We are changing racially. By the year 2040, whites will be a minority in the United States. Those who are desperately trying to halt any further structural change within organized religions are frustrated in their inability to squelch the current momentum. A religious response to the changing culture is not to resist change but to call a diverse people to a solidarity that is God-centered.

H. Richard Niebuhr in his classic work *Christ and Culture* clearly points out that over the centuries there have been five different approaches that Christians have taken in responding to the culture. The first is to have nothing to do with the culture. This strategy calls for a total loyalty to Christ without any concern for any culture since they are all transitory. The second response is to try to bring about a marriage between religion and culture, hoping that one will enhance the other. The third is to situate religion within the culture but clearly subordinating society to religion. The fourth method is to underscore the tension that should exist between religion and culture. The final option is to view religion as an instrument for transforming the culture.[4]

Niebuhr's second category would describe most of our immigrant parents and grandparents. They came to America to be a part of the culture. Most of their religious traditions have been accepted and absorbed into American culture. Conversely, in a relatively short period of time, the culture infiltrated the churches. This becomes problematic as our society shifts more heavily to secular and materialistic values.

Right now we live in a culture filled with stress because of the heavy demands that are placed upon us. We are a consumer society. We measure our success by how much we have and how much we plan on getting. The following anecdote illustrates our obsession with all the latest fads:

> I did as I was told. I was fussy about my peanut butter, fought cavities, became depressed over yellow wax build up. I was responsible for my husband's underarm being protected for twelve hours. I was responsible for making sure my children had a well-balanced breakfast. I alone was carrying the burden for my dog's shiny coat. We believed if we converted to all the products that marched before our eyes we could be the best, the sexiest, the freshest, the cleanest, the thinnest, the smartest and the first in our block to be regular. Purchasing for the entire family was the most important thing I had to do.[5]

Madison Avenue dictates the pace and standards of our living. Often we deceive ourselves into thinking that we proclaim God's Reign and that God's way establishes the pattern of our lives. Instead, without even realizing it, we are held captive by our culture and its standards. What's needed now is Niebuhr's fifth category: to live alternative values within the culture in order to transform it.

One way of doing this is through the coincidence of opposites. This approach can help transform our culture by blending seemingly opposing values. For example, materialism can be subordinated by a spiritualism that places material goods within their proper perspective. Individualism coupled with community can bring about a healthy balance between contemplation and relationships. Instead of absorbing the values of the culture, we need to live our values within it. A synthesis and proper ordering of these values can help bring about the Reign of God in the marketplace.

The Jews in the Hebrew Scriptures often had to create a coincidence of opposites as they faced foreign cultures. For example, in establishing a monarchy the Jews had to redefine what it meant to be a king. In surrounding cultures, being a king was tantamount to being a god. The Hebrews had to incorporate their monotheism into the institution of kingship to create a mode of leadership consistent with their faith experience.

The early church had to confront similar issues in its culture. Like the case of our immigrant ancestors, the first impulse expressed in the Letter to the Romans was to adapt to the culture. In the space of a generation, the culture had deteriorated to such a degree that the author of Revelation exhorted the people to get out of their ruts and to challenge the culture. The coincidence of opposites proposes that doing this would not only further God's Reign but also bring out the best in the culture.

Living in the Fast Lane

Because we often choose to plug into the culture, we live stressful lives like everyone else around us. I remember once walking along the streets of New York, bumping into people, racing along, fearful and frazzled. A man suddenly yelled out, "You're all crazy." I thought to myself, "He's right. Look at the way we are running around these streets."

Not too long ago, I was at St. Patrick's Cathedral for an ordination liturgy. As I was sitting in the sanctuary, the back doors of the cathedral flew open and I noticed the beautiful statue of Atlas across the street. As I looked over the prostrate bodies of those being ordained, I noticed how burdened Atlas looked, carrying the world on his shoulders. He is a symbol for the contemporary human being, burdened, bent over, and filled with stress.

Every time I celebrate the liturgy, I conclude by saying, "Go in peace." And often what follows is anything but peaceful. Sometimes I want to end by saying, "On your mark, get set, go," and shooting a gun in the air. We're off and running. And we don't even realize it half the time.

We've become so accustomed to living life in the fast lane, we don't even know that we are there. To illustrate this, I often tell the story of the grammar school I attended. Whenever we heard a siren, we stopped what we were doing and said the Hail Mary. This was followed by, "Sacred Heart of Jesus and our dear Blessed Mother, save and protect all of those in danger." The only problem was that our school was across from a hospital, the police department, and the volunteer fire squad. So we heard sirens all day. And we prayed all day, and I mean *all day*. To this day, whenever I hear a siren, I go through this whole routine. It certainly proves Pavlov's dog theory.

One day I was driving along the highway. I heard a siren and so I started my prayers. I continued to hear the siren, so I figured this must be pretty serious. So I said a second Hail Mary, and just as I was concluding my "Sacred Heart of Jesus and our dear Blessed Mother...," I saw the lights flashing in my rear-view mirror. The cop was chasing me for speeding. He was furious when he caught up with me. "What do you have to say for yourself?" "Officer," I told him, "you wouldn't believe it if I told you." He said, "I've been on the force for a lot of years. I've heard them all." I recounted my story. He said, "You're right, this is unbelievable. I'm not going to give you a ticket. If you are saying all of these prayers, that is very admirable. If you just made this story up, it's the best one I've heard in all my years."

I heard another story that I suspect might be exaggerated but is nevertheless certainly worth repeating. There was a man streaking, stark naked, running up and down the aisles of St. Patrick's Cathedral. The old rector, so preoccupied with the details of administration, caught up with the man and scolded him: "Sir, we do not allow running in the aisles of St. Patrick's. Please walk."

So often we are speeding along, and we don't even realize what's going on around us. We are filled with stress and aren't even aware of it. It's become a way of life. That's one of the major reasons why there are so many heart attacks and ulcers in our culture. Many of our illnesses are stress-related. God knows, the marketplace is filled with stress. The physician Robert Anderson wrote that he used to believe that 30 to 40 percent of the problems presented by patients were stress-induced. Now he thinks stress may be implicated in 90 percent of ailments.[6]

The Warning Signals

The body does not lie. Because so many of us are immune to the fact that we are stressed, it becomes imperative that we learn to pay attention to the body. Look to the signals that indicate that you have crossed over the line from health to the stress zone.

Loss of sleep and appetite are usually signs that something is wrong. Compulsive behaviors, such as excessive alcohol consumption, gambling, drug use, overeating, and sexual fixations are symptomatic of deeper issues. Through these behaviors the inner psyche is yelling out: "Please pay attention. Get some help."

If you find yourself not thinking clearly, overeating, and losing control, then ask yourself, "Why?" Notice also mood swings and other feeling manifestations such as depression, loneliness, anger, and excessive tiredness. These feelings are telling you that you are not doing a good job of managing your life and changes need to be made.

There are usually underlying attitudes at the root of these physical and emotional manifestations. A common one is perfectionism. Things have to be done a certain way. It's my way or no way at all. People who fall into this category always feel that things are not good enough and frequently think, "If it's going to be done right, I must do it myself." I think of Jack when I think about perfectionism. He was a vice-president on Wall Street. His whole life revolved around work. Everything had to be perfect. He was hard on himself and a slave driver to all those around him. People felt stressed just to be in same room with Jack. He got a lot done because people feared him. His whole life was the corporation. He had no social or family life. When mergers began to happen among the Wall Street banks, Jack was one of the first to be laid off. He's been unemployed for two years. I asked him recently, "Jack, if you had to do it over again, what would you change?" He said, "I would relax a little more. I would try to be a little less perfect and a little more human." Fortunately, Jack has time left in his life to change his behavior and live a happier life.

Complaining is another attitude that can underlie our compulsive behaviors. If you want to find the downside of life, you'll find it. There's always something wrong and things could be done better. It's the old story of the glass half empty or half full. The optimist wakes up and says, "Good morning, God." Meanwhile the pessimist says, "Good God, morning." The optimists bring joy wherever they go, while the pessimists bring happiness whenever they go.

The parents of the optimist and the pessimist decided to try to cure their children at Christmas time. They bought the pessimist a room full of toys and the optimist a room full of manure. When Christmas morning came, they went to the pessimist's room only to find him sitting in a corner. "What's the matter," they said. "I'm afraid to play with these toys. I might fall or get cut. It's safer to sit and watch." The frustrated parents left and went to the see how the optimist was doing. When they got to her room, she was throwing manure up in the air, making little manure pies, and just having the time of her life. "What are you doing?" they exclaimed. She gleefully responded, "With this much manure around, there must be a pony under this pile!" I'm not saying we should go around looking for ponies. People like that can be a bit much. However, a positive attitude can uplift a group and help them move beyond their stress. A complainer brings the whole group down with comments like, "I'm sick of this place," or "Why am I always the one who gets stuck with this?" If I find myself consistently being like this or talking like this, then chances are I'm not dealing too well with the stress in my life.

Finally, judgmental attitudes also create unhealthy behaviors. There is much psychological truth in the Gospel dictate not to judge others. After reading the Lord's words on making judgments, my friend Robert and I agreed that we would no longer judge. Instead we would only "take note." But whatever we call it, it's an attitude that produces anxiety. If I go around judging, then I am not relaxed in the way I walk about life. I'm carrying a burden because I see only the bad in others: "What an idiot!" "Where did they find her?" "What does he know?" These kinds of observations do not make for a pleasant life for myself or those around me. Often, judgmental people cloak their attitude behind a veneer of holiness. They present themselves as the pious, holier-than-thou types. I think of Fr. Marcellus. I lived with him for about five years. He had judgments and comments about everything, from what people were wearing to what time they came in at night. Of course, he never said these things directly. It was always by innuendo or couched in some pious platitude. He was so uptight that he seemed to be perpetually constipated. Whenever he was not home, the whole house could breathe.

It's inevitable that if I am stressed, I will bring stress to others. Chances are that if you are feeling stressful, it is because you are plugging into the culture. My stress is a sign that I am not an instrument of God's Reign. Something is wrong in my life and with my values. Although it's hard to change attitudes and behaviors, the alternative is worse.

Becoming Outrageously Happy

Linus said to Charlie Brown one day, "What do you want to be when you grow up?" Charlie Brown hesitated a bit and said, "When I grow up, I want to be outrageously happy." If there is one goal that every human being shares in common, it is to be happy. The problem is that people are sharply divided on how to get happy. In our culture, becoming rich, holding on to power, preventing war by preparing for war are our ambitions. I have suggested that all of these lead to a stress-filled existence. Ultimately, they do not make us outrageously happy. The way that Jesus has shown us in the Sermon on the Mount places stress where it belongs, among the arrogant, the greedy, and the war makers. Their lives and goals are absolutely incompatible with the beatitudes. Conversely, his way offers exorbitant felicity to those courageous enough to walk away from the promised pot of gold offered at the end of the corporate rainbow.

Jesus' sermon about happiness presents an understanding of living a stress-free life different from what we have been taught in our culture. His is the way of the Reign of God. Jesus is the model of the happy person. One of the consequences of his way of living was that it led to the cross. Recently I was in a card store and saw a card that was probably intended to be disrespectful. There was a sketch of Jesus on the cross and TGIF was inscribed on the crossbeam instead of the usual INRI. I said to myself, "Yes, thank God for Good Friday. It cost Jesus a lot, but it teaches us volumes."

Jesus was a peaceful man. He dealt well with stress. He led a balanced life. He noticed the lilies of the field and counted hairs on people's heads. He went to dinners with his friends, embarked on many fishing journeys, and when the apostles got to be too much for him, he ran away up to the mountains to pray and be alone with God. He had the sense and ability to recognize the stressful moments in his life and transform them into peaceful energy.

But he did place stress where it needed to be placed. He challenged religious, political, and economic leaders. His message made them nervous and stressful. They felt uncomfortable. Jesus' message about the equality and dignity of every human being threatened to turn the whole power structure upside down. It was their fear that put Jesus on the cross. And the cross is precisely the coincidence of opposites in its most powerful form. On the cross Jesus brought together heaven and earth, the vertical and horizontal. In his dying came resurrection. His message in the beatitudes is the message of the coincidence of opposites. The challenge of the beatitudes was too threatening for those people who would eventually crucify Christ. At the very moment of his death, when Jesus was most powerless, he was the most powerful. In that moment he transformed the world by turning its values upside down.

Who's Who in the Reign of God

There are two versions of the beatitudes in the New Testament. Matthew has eight beatitudes and Luke has four. Let's begin with Luke. Luke writes about who is happy from a Gospel perspective, whereas Matthew expounds on how to become happy.

Luke's version goes as follows:

> Blessed are you poor,
> for the kingdom of God is yours.
> Blessed are you who are now hungry,
> for you will be satisfied.
> Blessed are you who are now weeping,
> for you will laugh.
> Blessed are you when people hate you,
> and when they exclude and insult you,
> and denounce your name as evil
> on account of the Son of Man.
> Rejoice and leap for joy on that day!
> Behold, your reward will be great in heaven.
> For their ancestors treated the prophets in the same way.
> But woe to you who are rich.
> for you have received your consolation.
> But woe to you who are filled now,
> for you will be hungry.
> Woe to you who laugh now,

for you will grieve and weep.
Woe to you when all speak well of you,
for their ancestors treated the false prophets
in this way. (Luke 6:20–26)

Luke's beatitudes are addressed to those who are poor,
marginated, and rejected by the Jewish establishment. He is
eminently clear that God's Reign is for them. It is not a fu-
turistic reign but one in which they will begin to experience
God's peace, freedom, and justice right here and now. The
Reign of God is not exclusively for them, but they will have
special reason for rejoicing. They, especially, will experience its
promises.

What does this mean? Let me share an early childhood experience to illustrate Luke's point. I grew up in the city. We did
not lack the necessities of life, but we didn't have much beyond
them. One summer a wealthy donor enabled all of the children in our neighborhood to go away for two weeks to summer
camp. We had the time of our lives. We had access to beautiful
swimming pools, horseback riding, canoeing, archery, state-of-
the-art sports equipment, and luxurious accommodations. At
the end of two lavish weeks, the only payment we had to make
was to offer twenty hours of service in tutoring and helping
"less fortunate" children.

The camp was a lesson in equality. Rich and poor had access
to the same conveniences. The camp, however, was especially
for us poor children. The wealthy always had access to the
kind of things the camp offered. The reminder that there were
children less fortunate than we were was a challenge for us to
change our way of seeing the world. The lesson was that we
were all equal, and regardless of economic status, we all had
something that we could share.

And so it was with the poor in Luke's beatitudes. Jesus gives
them status. The blind, deaf, and poor were often considered to
be sinners and social outcasts. In restoring their health, Jesus restored their dignity and pride. At the same time, he called them
to conversion away from their sin and negativity.

The woes are addressed not necessarily to those who are materially rich. The woes are for people who unnecessarily accumulate possessions and do not share their resources with others. This kind of behavior is incompatible with the Reign of God.

Money as a form of economic exchange was introduced into Western civilization to facilitate the exchange and distribution of goods. Money should be the medium used to serve one another. It should make giving less cumbersome. Instead of the bulkiness of livestock and bags of grain and carts of vegetables, we have coins and bills to interact and share with one another. Unfortunately, money has often become the medium for injustice and inequality. Money properly used can be an instrument for community, equality, and reconciliation. Woe to those who use it for any other purpose. There is no room for them in God's Reign.

Lady Poverty

Matthew's emphasis is on the attitudes needed for the Reign of God. His list is truly a coincidence of opposites. He brings contradictory elements together in order to create a new energy for the transformation of the world.

> Blessed are the poor in spirit,
> for theirs is the reign of heaven.
> Blessed are they who mourn,
> for they shall be comforted.
> Blessed are the meek,
> for they will inherit the land.
> Blessed are they who hunger and thirst for righteousness,
> for they shall be satisfied.
> Blessed are the merciful,
> for they shall be shown mercy.
> Blessed are the clean of heart,
> for they will see God.
> Blessed are the peacemakers,

for they will be called children of God.
Blessed are they who are persecuted
for the sake of righteousness,
for theirs is the reign of heaven.
Blessed are you when they insult you and persecute you
and utter every kind of evil against you
because of me.
Rejoice and be glad, for your reward will be great in heaven.
Thus they persecuted the prophets who were before you.

                                        (Matt. 5:3–12)

Poverty of spirit is at the heart of Matthew's beatitudes. The
kind of poverty that he calls us to was clearly illustrated by
Lucy, a good friend, who almost drowned in the ocean. She was
enjoying the beach during a week of summer vacation. It was
a sunny day, and the ocean appeared to be calm. The waves
were gentle and inviting. She had swum about fifty feet away
from the shore when she got caught in an undercurrent. She
was fighting desperately for her life. The more she fought, the
more she lost her breath. Finally she just lay back, threw her
arms back and began to float. She prayed, "Lord, do with me
whatever you will." At that moment a great peace came over
her. The current passed and she safely made her way back to
the shore.

   She has since become a model for me in what it means to be
poor in spirit. Matthew's first beatitude, "Blessed are the poor
in spirit, for theirs is the reign of heaven," is at the heart and
foundation of the holiness. It means surrendering to God's way,
letting go of our need to be in control. It is declaring our dependence on God. The *anawim* were the people who did this in the
Hebrew Scriptures. Their material poverty was a sacrament of
their true inner poverty of spirit.

   This is the poverty of daily life. We can easily get lost in
the illusion that life on this planet is permanent. We can forget who we really are and where we are really going. St. Francis
began his conversion process by praying, "Who are you, God,
and who am I?" To know who we are in relationship to God

is the poverty of daily life. Life is fragile. I remember once having a little too much wine at a New Year's Eve party with some friends. I toasted everyone at midnight by saying, "We're all dying." To this day, friends tease me that I'm really a great one to have at a party. What's unnerving is that the toast is true. The tenuousness of our lives is our deepest poverty.

Luke's poverty is more of a material poverty, while Matthew's is more of an interior quality. Christian poverty has to be both. At its core, poverty liberates. This freedom enables the Christian to be close to those who are sociologically poor. There is a solidarity with them in their plight and a desire to share the spirit of our material and inner freedom. We share a common vision of detachment from prestige and power, the fear of insecurity and criticism, and the reluctance to take risks and throw discretion to the wind.

The church's credibility rests on its ability to witness to a radical poverty of spirit that includes but goes far beyond material poverty. The church should have only one reason to have money, possessions, and power: to share these with the poor. Its ministers and hierarchy especially must never seek wealth and power. Jesus gave us an example of what it means to be poor in spirit by washing the feet of his disciples. He let go of all status. He took on the role of a servant. Letting go of status means that distinctions among us are abolished. It always strikes me when papal honors are bestowed in a diocese that rarely are there any poor, homeless, or destitute who receive these honors. I am not suggesting that the rich be excluded. I am proposing that the poor be included since they are clearly God's favorites. They are the ones God honors. The only title that should be given any clergy is that of servant. It seems to me that is what Jesus asked us to do: "If I your Lord and master can be a servant so too must you be washers of one another's feet" (John 13:1–13).

Poverty of spirit is the surest pathway to God. This truth was underscored in a thirteenth-century Franciscan allegory, "The Holy Exchange." It is a story in which the brothers go into the world seeking Lady Poverty. Avarice is the obstacle to finding Lady Poverty, the chief obstacle in the spiritual journey. Lady Poverty leads the brothers up a mountain. It is a long, hard struggle. They are pilgrims all along the way. When they get to the top of the mountain, St. Francis and Lady Poverty are wedded. It is this union that leads St. Francis to intimacy with Christ.

Lady Poverty teaches us that we are pilgrims and strangers in this world. As pilgrims, we never have a secure resting place. We are always on our way, never fully arrived. The state of pilgrimage invites us to travel together, to solicit and welcome strangers along the way, and never to exclude anyone from our company. Poverty becomes our Lady, not because she is an end in herself but because she leads us to one another and brings us into the warm embrace of the poor man on the cross, who leads us to true riches and our enduring home.[7]

One day I was with my ninety-year-old mother. Each time I am with her these days, I am reminded of her frailty. Each week she is a little bit weaker. I keep wondering, "How much longer?" She has had her struggles along the way. She seems so ready to die. She who has been poor and faithful is ready to meet her God. I ask myself, "Why am I not ready to let her go?" Maybe it's because she is poor in spirit, and I'm not.

Freud wrote that the basic desire is the desire for life. Death threatens that basic desire. Because of the reality of death, many human desires are ultimately frustrated. The acceptance of this fact is life's key lesson. The sign of maturity is the ability to integrate the coincidence of opposites of the reality of death within the dreams of life. The acceptance of our mortality is the key to being truly poor in spirit. It is the great equalizer. People like my mother, who accepted little deaths all along the way, who lived life with open arms, approach the final death in exactly that way. Truly poor in spirit, their arms continue to stay opened, and they say, "Come, Sister Death, I love you. People are afraid of you because they do not understand you. Sister Death, I love you." Truly poor, now truly rich.

Mourning and Hungering

Matthew's "Blessed are they who mourn, for they will be comforted" and "Blessed are those who hunger and thirst for righteousness, for they will be satisfied" are reflections of Isaiah's words written centuries earlier: "Comfort my people and speak tenderly to Jerusalem" (Isa. 40:1).

Before we can give comfort to others, we must first change by redirecting our desires. The word that Matthew uses in Hebrew for mourning actually means a willingness to change. To adjust the way we do things and to change the things that we hunger after is very difficult. Values and visions are ingrained deep within us.

Recently I had the opportunity to visit Ellis Island. It was a very moving experience because my parents came to the United States from Rome through Ellis Island in 1921. I never realized what an ordeal it was for them. The documentation now made public at Ellis Island shows boatloads of immigrants being herded to America like cattle. They slept in dormitories, had little to eat, and wore shabby clothes. When they arrived in New York after weeks of being tossed around on a boat, they were assembled into long lines like school children to begin the process of entering the country. They had little money, owned few possessions, and were forbidden to have the security of a job before arriving. It is understatement to say that they were reduced to a subhuman status. When I asked my parents why they went through all of this, they always gave the same answer, "So we and our children could have a good life." A good life to them did not necessarily mean material prosperity. It did mean having the basic necessities of life and a good education, but above all it meant living with dignity and freedom.

We have been blessed to bear the fruits of the sweat and toil of our ancestors. We have lived the good life far beyond their initial dreams. For example, I have never experienced hunger or the anxiety of not having the basic necessities of life. Beyond this, I have known a level of comfort and educational advancement that would not have even entered my parent's minds as they journeyed across the ocean.

The statistics paint a shocking picture. We who comprise only 6 percent of the world's population use over 60 percent of its resources. The truth is that it is nice and feels good to have all of these things at our disposal. Right now, as the world economy is shifting, we Americans seem to be willing to do anything to maintain all that we have. There is little talk of embracing a national austerity plan and learning to live a more disciplined life where we learn to be content with less. That is the gridlock within many of our psyches. This is what needs to change. Each of us needs to begin by taking an inventory of personal items that need to change and then working toward structural and institutional reformation.

We need to redirect our hungers so that all people can have the opportunities for dignity and freedom that we have. It's important that we change our dreams and reimage our world. As our ancestors dreamed on the boats leading them to America, it is now time once again to dream new dreams. Our culture emphasizes success and achievement, while the beatitudes call us to dream and hunger for a better world. God tells David that it was all right that he did not achieve his goal of building the temple. "You did well that it was in your heart" (1 Kings 8:18). We need to look within our hearts and redirect our energies.

The task that remains is to take our renewed dreams and try our best to make them happen for the sake of those in our world who are waiting for relief from physical deprivations and emotional discrimination. There is an old Indian story that tells us what we need to do:

> It was nine o'clock in the morning and Nasruddin was fast asleep. The sun had risen in the sky, the birds were chirping in the trees and Nasruddin's breakfast was getting cold. So his wife woke him up.
>
> He woke up in a towering rage. "Why did you wake me up just now," he shouted. "Could you not have waited a little longer?"

"The sun has risen in the sky," said his wife, "the birds are chirping in the trees and your breakfast is getting cold."

"Foolish woman!" said Nasruddin, "Breakfast is a trifle compared to the contract of a hundred thousand gold pieces I was about to sign!"

So he turned over and tossed about in bed for a long time, attempting to recapture his shattered dream and his lost contract.

Now it so happened that Nasruddin was cheating in that contract and his business partner was an unjust tyrant.

If, on recapturing his dream, Nasruddin gives up his cheating, he will become a saint.

If he works strenuously to free the people from the oppression of the tyrant he will become a reformer.

If, in the midst of his dream, he suddenly realizes that he is dreaming, he will become an Awakened man and a Mystic.

Of what use is it to become a saint and a reformer if one is still asleep?[8]

Bernard Lonergan once wrote that it is not the theologians who will reform the church but the saints.[9] The saints are the blessed of whom Matthew writes. They have been awakened and enlightened and have redirected their dreams to bring about the Reign of God by giving comfort to those most in need.

The Power in Gentleness

At first, "Blessed are the gentle for they will inherit the land" might seem like Christians are called to be like melba milk toast and doormats. The coincidence of opposites is epitomized in this beatitude. One has to be really strong and secure in oneself in order to be gentle. This is not a beatitude for the wishy-washy and faint-hearted. There is a real power in gentleness.

Our lives are filled with violence. I don't mean the obvious violence, like gun killings, rapes, child molestation, and robberies. I mean the more subtle acts of violence that are just as much a part of daily life as that morning cup of coffee. In the marketplace we often view others as competitors to be defeated so that we might advance. It is violent to see others as objects rather than as human beings, God's children.

Our very system of education breeds this kind of violence. I experience this in many graduation addresses given by adult students. Frequently, their message is that now that they have a degree they can compete in the business world. They will be eligible for promotions and salary raises. To me, this is violent thinking. Our system is one that teaches that in order to get ahead, we need to rival the people around us. The very nature of competing means that I must win and someone else must lose. Often, all that matters is the winning. How one gets there is secondary. This attitude is not only brutal; it is unjust.

On a level that is very close to home, what about the way we drive our cars? Often we are reckless, disobeying speed limits and other traffic laws. Even more basic than this is the lack of courtesy on the road. We yell, shout, and curse at one another. Just yesterday as I was driving along the highway, two old ladies were in the car behind me. I couldn't believe my eyes when one of them gave me the finger because I forgot to put on a directional signal. Even the nicest people, even little old ladies, become violent behind a steering wheel.

To live nonviolently in a violent world is a difficult task. I believe that there is a real power in gentleness. Fr. Martin taught me that lesson in high school. We had a lot of respect for him. He was a man of integrity and the highest personal standards. I'll never forget the time that a few of us were smoking cigarettes in the lavatory during a school dance. When Fr. Martin walked into the room, we quickly stamped our cigarettes out on the floor. The smoke-filled air was a dead giveaway. Without saying a single word, Fr. Martin, dressed in his long robes, bent down, picked up the cigarette butts off the floor and threw them into the trash can. He looked at us, smiled, and walked out the door. He never said another word. And we never again smoked in the lavatory.

His kindness taught us a lesson that day. There is an eloquence and authority in nonviolence. On a larger scale, Gandhi taught the world that same lesson. He conquered by nonresistance. Even in those instances where we might judge force necessary, it should always be motivated by love and administered with gentleness. Oppression and violence may win the battle but never the war. People respect those who walk with a firm gentleness in the midst of hostility, greed, and chaos. To these belong the earth and its fullness.

Like Sipping Espresso

Shakespeare captured the essence of "Blessed are the merciful" when he wrote, "The quality of mercy is not strain'd. It droppeth as the gentle rain from heaven upon the place beneath. It blesseth him that gives and him that takes."[10] More than anything else, mercy is an interior attitude, a personality trait that has to be acquired. Becoming merciful is something that evolves slowly and quietly. I went with a friend recently to a coffee bar. We both ordered espresso. He gulped his down. Espresso is not supposed to be drunk that way. Slowly, gradually, its strong taste is meant to be savored. The mercy that the Lord speaks about is like espresso. It's so strong and important for community that it has to be absorbed bit by bit.

The word "mercy" is rooted in the Hebrew 'hesed, meaning graciousness, kindness, and acceptance. We get a hint of its meaning from the prophet Hosea. In this beautiful book of the Hebrew Scriptures, the allegory of a husband's faithful love toward an unfaithful wife is used to symbolize 'hesed, God's unconditional love for Israel.

The very nature of mercy means that it is not necessarily deserved and must be freely given, with no strings attached. It is much more than compassion. Compassion can be given at a distance between the one giving and the one receiving.

Mercy implies solidarity, a unity and equality. It is a letting go of protocol and agendas. Communities that will endure must be built upon this generous self-giving and self-forgetting. The very mission of the church is to create these kinds of communities, calling people to a brotherly and sisterly 'hesed. Creating communion is not achieved at the snap of one's fingers. It is an invitation to a long and even painful growth process.

The story of the Good Samaritan is the clearest example in the New Testament of what is meant by mercy. Samaritans were outcast Jews. They were looked upon as being low class. In the story, the people that were expected to stop and help the person in need did not do so. It was the Samaritan, the outcast, who came closest to God's gift of 'hesed. The openness and letting go of preconceived characterizations demanded by this parable invites heroic character depth and immeasurable conviction.

The closest experience I have had of this parable occurred when I was stationed in Yonkers, New York. I lived in a rectory on top of a hill. I had to travel down the hill into the poor section of town to get over to the seminary where I was teaching. It was a below-zero winter day. As I was driving, I saw a very old woman wearing only a sweater pacing back and forth carrying two shopping bags. My heart ached for her. I thought to myself that if she were my mother, I would hope someone would stop and help her. I wished that I could, but I was already late for my class. I felt like the priest in the Good Samaritan story, who couldn't help the person in need because of his religious obligations.

While I was teaching my class, all I could think of was this woman. To my great surprise, on my way home after class, she was still standing there in the cold. I thought, "Here's my chance." I stopped the car and said, "Please get in. I'll give you a ride." The woman got into the car and slammed the door. After a few seconds of silence, I said, "What's your name?" She quickly responded, "That's really none of your business." I asked her where she wanted to go. She responded by telling me to make left and right turns. I followed her instructions. After about an hour of this, I realized that she was taking me along the bus route. A trip that should have taken about ten minutes took over an hour. I thought to myself, "I know that this story will have a happy ending. It will be like something in *Catholic Digest*. She is probably a rich old lady who will give me a sizeable check for the church when I drop her off." When we got to a diner, she abruptly said, "Stop the car and pull over." She got out of the car and slammed the door. No good-bye and no check.

I was furious. I was angrier still when I got home and found myself in trouble with the pastor for being late for dinner. I was fuming all night long. I sat with my anger the next morning, trying to figure it out. It suddenly dawned on me that I was attempting to be kind to this woman. I saw her as a poor thing. I thought that I was better because I was well educated, well dressed, and well mannered. What I lacked was the quality of mercy that is an equalizer among persons. I had no desire to be in communion or solidarity with this woman, to truly call her "sister." God's *'hesed* is unconditional. It makes no comparisons between persons and doesn't look for gratitude in return for favors. Mercy abandons all distinctions, knows no bounds, and creates a true human family that will endure.

Sincerely Yours

Have you ever stopped to think about the meaning of the words "sincerely yours," which concludes many letters written and received? The word "sincere" comes from the two Latin words *sine* and *cere,* which means "without wax." The origin of the word came from Roman correspondence. A waxed seal was placed over important documents. A letter sent without wax was one in which nothing was hidden, one that could be read openly. Someone who is sincere is "without wax," open and up front. What you see is what you get.

The sixth beatitude, "Blessed are the pure of heart," is the one that points the way to experiencing God. The deeper meaning of this beatitude is the call to purify one's motives, to become truly sincere. In T. S. Eliot's *Murder in the Cathedral,* Thomas receives three visitors, representing three temptations. It was no problem for him to overcome them all. The fourth visitor points out to Thomas that he is much too strong a man to be overcome by these other three. He tells Thomas that the only road open to him is to become a martyr. He describes for Thomas the shrine that would be built in his honor and how pilgrims would come to visit the shrine. Thomas recognizes the fourth temptation as the most subtle of all. The last temptation is the greatest treason: to do the right deeds for the wrong reasons.

Maybe there is no such thing as absolutely pure motivation. Sigmund Freud taught that we do everything for pleasure. William Adler disagreed with Freud. He taught that it wasn't pleasure but power that most forcefully gripped us. From their viewpoint, life is a series of manipulations, maneuvering for pleasure, power, or control.

Even though most of us would take exception with Freud and Adler, we would have to admit that there are elements of truth in their teachings. We need to constantly ask ourselves, "Why do I do the things that I do?" Chances are that we will find that our motives are not totally pure. That's okay, as long as we are aware of that reality. We then need to change attitudes and behaviors so that we are not using other human beings simply to satisfy our needs. From a Christian viewpoint, God's grace can purify our mixed motives so "that all things work unto the good" (Rom. 8:28).

The biblical notion of purity of heart is one that invites the letting go of false gods in order to worship the one true God. The gods of my life are those things, events, goals, or persons with which I am obsessed. Often we are unaware of the false gods that we worship. A good way to get in touch with these is to ask such questions as, "How do I spend my time?" "What do I daydream about?" "What do I dream about at night?" "Where does most of my energy go?" The answers to these questions will give some hints about the gods that we worship.

Purifying our motives leads to the removal of the masks that we wear. Once I kneel naked, masks removed, then and only then do I have a chance of experiencing the real God. Masks are the single most significant obstacles to finding God in our lives. It's the old story of the peeling off of the layers of the onion in order to get to the core. Layers of impure motivation and insincerity disguised in ways that often we ourselves are unaware of prevent us from seeing ourselves, others, and even God as they really are.

Peacemakers

Peacemakers are the real children of God: "Blessed are the peacemakers, for they shall be called the children of God." The essence of becoming as a child in the seventh beatitude is to become an icon of God by bringing *shalom* into the world. Jesus came to reconcile, to make right relationships that had been broken among human beings and with God. The *shalom* that Jesus wished for the world before he died was a wholeness and an integrity that would be refreshing and renewing for the universe.

Children had no status in the time of Jesus. The invitation to become a child was not an attractive one. Being a child in first-century Palestine was to be an absolutely nonthreatening entity. And maybe that's what's needed to be a peacemaker. Letting go of vested interests and status is the only thing that will make people comfortable enough to lay aside their swords. Only children can create such a comfortable atmosphere.

The key word in this beatitude is "maker." Mother Jones had an insight into this when she wrote, "Pray for the dead, but work like hell for the living." Reconciliation doesn't happen simply by waving a magic wand. It takes a lot of hard work. In his efforts to bring reconciliation to a divided nation, Abraham Lincoln's motto was "Die when I may, I would like it said of me that I always pulled up a weed and planted a flower where

I thought a flower would grow."[11] When we make peace happen, the world becomes a more beautiful place, a place where children are comfortable and can freely play.

The task of the peacemaker is to take a little glimpse into heaven, see what's there, and then begin to make it happen here and now. Some people might view creating heaven as being unrealistic. The question is, "What is really real?" It reminds me of the time I was walking down the street dressed with a Roman collar. A woman looked at me and said, "Are you for real?" When I looked up at her, I noticed the false eyelashes, dyed hair, and a face covered with make up. So what's for real?

Creating a bit of heaven on earth is not to create a perfect world here and now. That's impossible. What it does mean is to take another look at what we call reality. The role of the peacemaker is to help redefine reality. Reality is as it is seen from God's eyes. From God's vantage point, *shalom* is reality.

Paying Your Two Bucks

An old friend always used to say, "You have to pay your two bucks." His message was that if you want to make things happen you have to be willing to pay the price. He captured for me the bottom line of the beatitudes: "Blessed are you when they insult you and persecute you and utter every kind of evil against you because of me. Rejoice and be glad, for your reward will be great in heaven. Thus, they persecuted the prophets who were before you."

The beatitudes offer us the opportunity to pay our dues to the right organization and for the right goals. A Jewish philosopher pointed out that there were three reasons why Christians fail: they love their enemies, they do not seek to possess the goods of the world, and they do not respond to violence with violence.

All that the beatitudes are about requires that we be willing to pay the two bucks to make them happen. When I was working on my doctoral dissertation, I used to use the library at Maryknoll School of Theology. I was fortunate that I happened to be there during Bishop James Walsh's last days. Although he had spent most of his life in prison in China, he was so peaceful, happy, and serene every time I saw him. His life in prison speaks powerfully about his character and his living out of the beatitudes. He certainly paid his two bucks. In doing so, he embodied the end result of those who live the attitudes of the beatitudes. He was truly light for the world. Cardinal Newman described well people like Bishop Walsh of Maryknoll, who have shown us that it is possible to live the beatitudes and be light for the world.

> Dear Jesus,
> help me to spread your fragrance
>   everywhere I go.
> Flood me with your spirit and life.
> Penetrate and possess my whole being
>   so utterly that my life may only be
>   a radiance of yours.
> Shine through me and be so in me
>   that every person I come in contact with
>   may feel your presence in my spirit.
> Let them look up and see no longer me
>   but only you, Lord Jesus.
> Stay with me and then I shall begin
>   to shine as you shine,
>   so as to be light to others.
> The light, O Jesus, will be all from you.
> None of it will be mine.
> It will be you shining on others through me.[12]

Conclusion

If we were to single out the one person in human history who most eloquently epitomized the beatitudes in bringing Christ's light into the world that person would be Mary. We even call her "Blessed Mother." The Magnificat is a wonderful expression of Mary's praise of God. She has seen the beatitudes fulfilled, the values of the world turned upside down, the co-incidence of opposites: "He has shown might with his arm, dispersed the arrogant of mind and heart. He has thrown down the rulers from their thrones but lifted up the lowly. The hungry he has filled with good things; the rich he has sent away empty" (Luke 1:46–55).

Mary spoke her *Fiat* to God's plan for her life. Despite the rejection by her culture symbolized in King Herod's plan to kill her child, Mary found peace and strength in living differently from many of the people of her times. She was truly as gentle as a dove and as cunning as a serpent in her ability to challenge people by her life and words: "Do whatever he tells you" (John 2:5).

Several months ago I was visiting Ein-Karen, the site of the visitation of the Blessed Mother to St. Elizabeth. As I sat on the stone wall overlooking the magnificent Galilean hills, I pictured these two pregnant women running to greet one another. I could only begin to imagine the degree of ecstasy that they felt. Two women, who counted for nothing in Jewish society, embracing one another and singing God's praises for God truly opted for the poor and lowly. God put down the mighty from their thrones in choosing these two insignificant people over the rich, the religious and political establishment of the day. All generations call her blessed (Luke 1:48) for although she did not always understand (Luke 2:50), she lived the contradiction of the beatitudes. She was a Coincidence of Opposites.

REFLECTION STARTERS

1. Make two columns. Write "dove" over the first and "serpent" over the second. Reflect or write specific ways you embody these symbols. After you have completed your lists, spend some time reflecting on how you might integrate these apparent opposites.

2. How much stress is in your life? Look over the following checklist to get some idea of your situation:

STRESS SIGNS AND SYMPTOMS

- back pain
- impatience
- stomach distress
- chronic fatigue
- letting more and more slip
- not feeling well
- tense facial muscles
- other physical ailments
- more resentment
- crying
- abruptness
- panic
- insomnia
- anxiety
- moodiness
- overeating
- overdrinking
- oversmoking
- oversleeping
- making a fuss over little things
- blaming
- irritability
- complaining
- rarely smiling
- sarcastic humor
- losing touch with friends
- procrastination
- feeling overwhelmed
- feeling out of control
- avoiding people
- losing sense of humor
- personality change

Spend some time evaluating your level of stress and make some decisions about what you're going to do to change attitudes and situations in your life.

3. Reflect on the gods you worship and the dreams and hungers that motivate you. To help you get in touch with these, draw a pie representing a typical twenty-four hour day. Divide the day into segments according to how you spend your time. Then think about the things you daydream about and the things that anger, annoy, and upset you. How we spend our time and what preoccupies us is a pretty clear indication of what or who we worship.

4. Reread Luke's and Matthew's version of the beatitudes. Imagine that Jesus were here today teaching these values. How would he speak them today? What examples and illustrations might he use? How would church and government leaders react to these teachings? How do you think your friends would respond? And finally, what about you?

CHAPTER SIX

Mystics in the Marketplace

The young salesman approached the farmer and began to talk excitedly about the book he was carrying. "This book will tell you everything you need to know about farming," the young man said enthusiastically. "It tells you when to sow and when to reap. It tells you about weather, what to expect and when to expect it. This book tells you all you need to know."

"Young man," the farmer said, "that's not the problem. I know everything that is in that book. My problem is doing it."

— As retold by Joseph Gosse

Focus Questions

- What's your Christ like? Human? Divine?

- What can Jesus and his message offer American culture?

- Name one of your addictions. What are you doing about it?

- Think of where you are in your spiritual journey. Reflect on where you would like to be. Choose one concrete action that you can do to help you grow.

Jesus Who?

For Christians, Jesus is the model for all that we are and all that we try to do. It is critical that we truly understand who the historical Jesus was and how we should apply his message for today. There is an alternative version of the Caesarea Philippi incident that did not make it into the New Testament canon:

> Jesus came with his disciples one day to Caesarea Philippi, and he said to them: "Who do people say I am?" And they said to him: "You are the Revealer." "You are the absolute, unsurpassable victory of God's self-bestowal." "You are the second person of the Blessed Trinity." "You are the unbroken contact with the Ground of Being." "You are the Man for Others." "You are the Word incarnate." "You are the prophetic manifestation of the eschaton." And Jesus said, "What?"[1]

The way we define Christ has a domino effect on all areas of our lives. In his book *The Last Temptation of Christ,* Nikos Kazantzakis puts his finger on the problem:

> The dual substance of Christ
> The yearning, so human,
> Superhuman of man to attain God
> has always been a deep
> inscrutable mystery to me.
> My principal anguish and source
> of all my joys and sorrows
> from my youth onward
> has been the incessant
> merciless battle between
> the spirit and the flesh.
> And my soul is the arena
> where the two armies have clashed and met.[2]

The issue of the relationship between the human and divine in Christ has plagued Christians for two thousand years. In the year 451, the Council of Chalcedon defined that Jesus was

truly God and truly human. There is a tension in that statement. How do you reconcile two conflicting traits? For the
next fifteen hundred years, many people in the church favored
the divinity component of the definition. The implication was
that Jesus was merely pretending to be human. But people still
struggled with the question of the relationship between the divinity and humanity of Christ. Some maintain the preference for
divinity, while others now emphasize the humanity of Christ.
The truth, however, lies in the tension of "fully human," "fully
divine."

I think that the struggle to revisit the Christology of Chalcedon is one of today's most important theological issues. I
personally experienced this when I returned to graduate school
in the 1980s. I had grown up with and fully accepted a notion
of Christ that favored his divinity. When I suddenly realized that
there were other ways of looking at the question, there was a
void in my life. I wasn't sure what to do with these questions
since until then I had thought there was only one way of looking
at Jesus.

I began to realize that Jesus was someone totally immersed in
his culture and that he shared human life to the fullest. Because
he did not sin, he was the most human person that ever lived.
When we choose sin, we choose to be less than human. Jesus
always chose and affirmed all that is human. This Jesus offers
freedom to the rest of us not only in the life to come but also in
life here and now. Jesus is not indifferent to the needs and concerns of the world. Jesus is the Savior who is also the Liberator
of humankind.

The starting point for encountering this Jesus is in the midst
of daily life. Jesus is present in the messiness of the marketplace.
The compelling attraction of this understanding of Jesus is at-
tested to in the popularity of the story "Footprints," which has
spread far and wide in only a few years.

One night a man had a dream. He dreamed he was walking along the beach with the Lord. Across the sky flashed
scenes from his life. For each scene, he noticed two sets of

footprints in the sand; one belonged to him, and the other to the Lord.

When the last scene of his life flashed before him, he looked back at the footprints in the sand. He noticed that many times along the path of his life there was only one set of footprints. He also noticed that it happened at the very lowest and saddest times in his life.

This reality bothered him and he questioned the Lord about it. "Lord, you said that once I decided to follow you, you'd walk with me all the way. But I have noticed that during the most troublesome times in my life, there is only one set of footprints. I don't understand why when I needed you most you would leave me.

The Lord replied, "My precious, precious child, I love you and I would never leave you. During your times of trial and suffering, when you see only one set of footprints, it was then that I carried you."[3]

The attraction that so many people have to this piece testifies that the human heart longs for a God who cares for us and carries us along the way. Jesus mirrors an image of God who is close to us and deeply involved with all that is human.

The historical Jesus treated every person as precious. When we strip the Gospel of a preconceived notion of the "sweet Jesus of Nazareth," we find a Christ who is in deep trouble for restoring dignity to women, children, sinners, the sick, and outcasts. If we accept a Christ who was really human, this has serious implications for Christians in the world. Just as Jesus dignified humanity and frees people in his world, we must now do the same for people in today's world.

In reading the Gospels, we note that Christ does not heal everyone. As Ralph Waldo Emerson once wrote, "There is a crack in everything God has made." There's always a part of life that remains broken. This is where the mystery of the divine enters. The fullness of healing, life, and freedom will happen only in heaven. The Christian, then, is one whose feet are firmly planted on the ground with eyes fixed on the life that is yet to

come. The Jesus who was so fully human challenges us to be totally immersed in the experience of life. The Christ who is God
is a sign that the best is yet to come. We live in the "in-between"
times, immersed in the concerns of daily life while waiting for
the fullness of life in heaven. The acceptance of the divinity of
Christ does not excuse us from complete involvement in the
marketplace. The affirmation of the humanity of Christ must
not allow us to forget that we are waiting for Christ to come
again at the end of time. That is the tension of the human and
divine in every human being.

Jesus in America

To press the issue further, we need to look at Jesus from the
vantage point of American culture. Who is Jesus and what
does his message mean for those of us living now in American society? I recently listened to a tape by a popular retreat
master. I was disgusted and depressed after listening. He had
absolutely nothing good to say about the United States. No
doubt about it: there are some very ugly trends in our culture. I
have already pointed out many of these. But there is also a lot
that is good. We must never forget that we are founded upon
a wonderful belief system that is profoundly religious at its
core. The Declaration of Independence epitomizes the American
spirit:

> We hold these truths to be self-evident, that all men are
> created equal and that they are endowed by their Creator
> with certain inalienable rights, that among these are life,
> liberty, and the pursuit of happiness. That to secure these
> rights, governments are instituted among men, deriving
> their just powers from the consent of the governed.

Even though the Declaration of Independence was written over
two hundred years ago, Jefferson, Franklin, and Washington
would recognize these values in the hearts of many Americans
today. Despite the hazards of the journey and rough beginnings

upon arrival in America, the early twentieth-century immigrants almost always found personal freedom, economic progress, and religious liberty. People possess these rights in the United States simply because they are human beings. This is a powerful legacy that has been given to us.

Part of our American immigrant tradition has been to constantly reacclimate itself to the world and its needs with the coming of each group to our soil. It is critical that we surface and deal with those trends that do not reflect values of God's Reign and the vision of the beatitudes. I think you will find that often there is a correlation between Gospel values and those of our founding fathers and mothers. These values are our legacy as Christians and Americans. It is our mission to uphold them. As Jesus confronted individuals and systems in his day, U.S. Christians must do the same in our culture today. I would identify a few areas that should concern us.

First and foremost, we need to confess any ways that we have taken advantage of the resources of developing countries. Dom Helder Camara once said to a visiting group of North Americans, "If you are appalled by what you see here, please don't try to start a revolution here. If you really want to help us, go back to your own country and work to change the policies of your government that exploit our country and keep our people so poor."[4]

His admonition is borne out by the fact that if the world were a village of one hundred people, seventy of them would be unable to read, over fifty would be suffering from malnutrition, and over eighty would live in what we call substandard housing. Of the hundred members of the global village, six would be Americans. These six would have one-half of the village's entire income and would consume one-third of the total energy resources available. Of the U.S. population less than 2 percent own 80 percent of the U.S. corporate wealth. We must refuse to accept any compromise that would suggest that this picture can in any way be compatible with the Gospel of Jesus.

Second, there is the issue of sexism. Religious people have often contributed to women's second-class status in our society.

Historically, women were not always treated with dignity, not only within religious denominations but even within marriages and the family structure itself. This is not the way Jesus treated women. The Gospels contain many examples where Jesus went beyond his religious culture in treating women with respect, dignity, and equality.

When a child was born in first-century Palestine, there was much rejoicing if it was a boy. If it was a girl, the family mourned instead of celebrating. There is absolutely no trace of this kind of prejudice in Jesus' ministry. In fact, we find the opposite. For example, in the Martha/Mary story (Luke 10:38–42), what is shocking about Mary's behavior is that only men were allowed to sit at a teacher's feet as disciples. Jesus is clearly breaking a religious tradition in order to affirm the equality and dignity of women.

Third, ageism is a byproduct of our death-denying society. We fear death and are terrified of old age. These are the worst things that can happen to an individual in our society. We touch up our hair, lift our faces, and even lie about our ages. Although families often have no other alternative, the growing number of nursing homes in the United States indicates that in some ways we have abandoned our elderly. It is too painful to be with the elderly because they are a stark reminder of the inevitable. We have become numb to this national insensitivity to old people. This became very obvious to me during a recent visit to Italy. The elderly are treated with deep reverence and respect for their wisdom and contributions to society. The fact that the elderly hold the highest place in the family structure in Italian culture presents a stark contrast to the status of our elderly.

Finally, racism continues to plague our nation and even our churches. Unfortunately, the situation seems to be getting worse rather than better. There is no need to prove that racial discrimination is absolutely contrary to the Gospel. Jesus welcomed Samaritans, who were discriminated against by most Jews. There is no way of proving the color of Jesus' skin. It is possible that he was dark-skinned, as were many Jews living in the Galilee region. Regardless of his skin color, there is no need to explain or document how Christians should treat people of other races. Every page of the Gospel speaks loudly and clearly to that issue.

Often our theology and spirituality are articulated and seen through the lens of the white middle class. We have to face the hard reality that many of our churches are places where blacks and other minorities are not always comfortable. Our way of praying, interacting, and singing reflects our white middle-class structures. I am not saying that is bad in itself. What I am saying is that we must examine ourselves for racist attitudes, repent of these, and change so that others will feel welcomed.

These are just four of the most obvious American issues that should be included in our Christology. In addition to these structural issues, we must not lose sight of emotional issues that plague many in our culture. Certainly, the miracles of Jesus demonstrate his ministry toward physical, spiritual, and emotional wholeness. We must try to identify sicknesses — mental, physical, and spiritual — that plague so many people in the United States.

It is so easy to forget the subtle areas of sickness of the middle class. Some suggest that there are three areas that captivate and blind middle-class people: (1) boredom: the general sense of nondirection, meaninglessness, and spiritual ennui that afflicts modern life; (2) alcohol and drugs: the chemical addictions by which so many seek to escape the pain of everyday life; (3) the tendency toward a prophylactic life: a life without risks, resting in our security.[5] These emotional, chemical, and attitudinal expressions are certainly manifestations that burden and chain down countless people in our culture.

These are some of the issues that we should study and begin to resolve. We should be filled with a sense of passion about the issues that confront our society. This is what it means to follow a Christ who was human and immersed in the concerns of the world around him. Christ's person and message can enhance, challenge, and develop our magnificent American legacy. It is the contribution of Christians in America to mediate the freedom of the Risen Jesus to today's men and women. For us to do anything less would be to settle for the "good old plastic Jesus" and a Christianity whose God is dead.

American Holiness

The Second Vatican Council gave us a compelling vision for using the Gospel to address the problems of today's world. In its Pastoral Constitution on the Church in the Modern World, the bishops declared:

> The joy and hope, the grief and anguish of the men of our time, especially those who are poor or afflicted in any way, are the joy and hope, the grief and anguish of the followers of Christ as well. Nothing that is genuinely human fails to find an echo in their hearts. For theirs is a community composed of men, of men who, united in Christ and guided by the Holy Spirit, presses onward toward the kingdom of the Father and are bearers of a message of salvation intended for all.[6]

When these words were written in 1965, Latin American theologians were writing about the gross injustices that were causing the death of humanity on that continent. Meanwhile, in the United States, the *New York Times* published an article entitled "New Theologians See Christianity without God." Even though they expressed it differently, people on both continents recognized that something was wrong.

In the United States, an awareness was emerging that traditional theological categories were no longer adequate to accommodate changing circumstances. The Latin American vantage point was the oppression of the poor. This became the Latin Americans' starting point for doing theology. They realized that ecclesial institutions had often aligned themselves with the wealthy class. The United States was still operating from a European model of doing theology that began not with human experience but with reflective thought. Despite the methodological difference, both North American and Latin American theologians realized that something had to change.

The difference in approach is not found in the critical reflection on the road traveled to reach understanding, but in the traveling itself. The Greek notion of wonder at God's justice, beauty, and truth is at the basis of European theology and motivates all knowing.[7] Since these attributes are not readily found in Latin America, the suffering of the present moment, not wonder, plays the active role in the process of understanding. The method originating in Latin America can be adapted to our culture to forge a new way for embarking on the spiritual journey and responding to at least some of the issues facing the world and church today. The Latin American approach coupled with our own tradition can offer an excellent tool for developing a spirituality in the marketplace according to the vision given by Vatican II.

The proposed method is not merely the developing of new themes. It is a another way of becoming holy in the marketplace. It begins with the experience of faith and then constructs a theology. It suggests an integration of human experience, theology, and spirituality. Theology is always at its best when it incorporates human experience and expresses itself in a spirituality. Conversely, spirituality is most solid when it is rooted in theology. The convergence of these various elements creates a vision of God and life that is truly relevant.

The spirituality of liberation proposes a critical reflection on human experience based on the teachings of Christ and the Christian tradition. Freedom is its goal in three areas: (1) the sociopolitical: freedom for all those who are oppressed and suffer from injustice in any way; (2) the human spirit: freedom from the addictions that impair human growth and development; (3) cosmic freedom: liberation from sin, the ultimate root of all injustice and oppression to provide for all people the opportunity for participation in community.

The starting point of this spirituality is conversion to neighbor, a commitment to the service of those who suffer any form of oppression. Juan Luis Segundo, one of the most erudite of the Latin American theologians, proposed the methodology of the hermeneutical circle to achieve these goals. The method involves the continuous change in our interpretation of the Bible, which is dictated by ongoing individual and societal developments. Underlying this process is a dissatisfaction with the way things are and a commitment to change that reality. New questions are applied to the biblical texts, which change our interpretation of the Scriptures. Segundo describes the method as follows:

> Firstly, there is our way of experiencing reality, which leads us to ideological suspicion. Secondly, there is the application of our ideological suspicion to the whole ideological superstructure in general and to theology in particular. Thirdly, there comes a new way of experiencing theological reality that leads to exegetical suspicion, that is, to the suspicion that the prevailing interpretation of the Bible has not taken important pieces of data into account. Fourthly we have our new hermeneutic, that is, our way of interpreting the fountainhead of our faith (i.e., Scripture) with the new element at our disposal.[8]

Segundo uses James Cone, the black theologian, to demonstrate the four stages of the hermeneutical circle. First, Cone begins by realizing that there is something wrong with any system that oppresses and excludes people. In paying attention to his experience, he notices this exclusion prevalent even within the church. This is the suspicion that begins the process of the hermeneutical circle. In examining his theological tradition, he notices that this system has primarily been transmitted by the white power structure. This is the second step of the process, in which theological premises are revisited. Thirdly, when he looks at the Scriptures from the black experience of slavery and oppression, he begins to find a new meaning in the Exodus event and the freedom that God gave to the Jews. Finally, he suggests that we need to enter into the black experience in order to fully understand the freedom God offers in the Exodus. The circle is now completed.

Segundo's point is not necessarily to endorse Cone's theology. He simply points out that Cone does a good job of using the hermeneutical circle to reinterpret Scripture and tradition in a way that speaks meaningfully to the black community. The use of this method to reinterpret God's word more authentically could be a powerful tool in resolving some of the social ills of our day.

Liberation theologians make it clear that changing our way of thinking must lead to a change of behavior. To carry this even further, some would say that a changed person in an unchanged system doesn't make much difference. Two other Latin American theologians, Leonardo and Clodovis Boff, propose a threefold method to facilitate the change of systems. First, they invite us to *see*. Look around and notice the things in our world that need changing. They suggest that we use the tools of the social sciences to accomplish this. Based on what we see, then we should *judge*. Make concrete judgments based on the Scriptures and the Christian tradition according to our perception of God's plan to change this situation. Finally, *act*. Come up with a plan of action, concrete ways to change what needs to be changed.[9]

The method is simple yet forceful. It can be applied to all areas of life. It has obvious implications for working with the poor in our cities. More subtly, in the business world it can be equally as strong. For example, if as a stockholder you happen to find out that a corporation is supportive of unjust personnel practices in developing countries, you can respond by making challenging choices. If upon reflecting on these unjust practices, it becomes clear to you that they are in opposition to the teachings of the beatitudes, you can choose actions such as informing other shareholders, writing letters to the corporation leaders, protesting verbally at shareholders meetings, or selling your stock.

This is a spirituality that moves beyond thoughts and feelings and expresses itself in action. The new heavens and new Jerusalem promised in the book of Revelation (21:2) can happen right here in the marketplace only when people who are hungry for justice are willing to pay the price to build this new city. Then the old earth filled with oppression will pass away and a new world will come to be where love, peace, and justice will truly reign.

Is it possible? The story is told of the wisest person who ever lived. A group of people wanted to prove this person a fool. They decided to bring a bird in hand to the wise person. They would ask the question, "Is this bird dead or alive?" If he said "dead," they would open their hands and allow the bird to fly away. If he said "alive," they would crush the bird in their hands. When they arrived, they said to the man, "Is this bird dead or alive?" He looked at them and said, "The answer to that question lies in your hands." Is it possible to create a new heaven and a new earth? The answer to that question lies in your hands.

Struck by Grace in the Marketplace

We used to talk about occasions of sin and the importance of avoiding persons, places, and things that could lead us into sin. I would like to suggest a more positive approach in which we look for moments of grace in the marketplace.

Every day there are persons, places, and things in the marketplace, sometimes in places where we would least expect, that can lead us closer to God. God offers us many opportunities to experience wholeness and holiness in the messiness of daily life. The experience of our own personal imperfection testifies to our need for God and others; it is our particular path to holiness. The imperfections and sinfulness of the world and its structures are an opportunity to inject change and new life so that people may experience an abounding freedom.

I would like to apply the principles of Alcoholics Anonymous as one way of paying attention to the opportunities for grace in the marketplace. I chose this particular spirituality because it is American. There are some who even think that the spirituality of Alcoholics Anonymous is the American contribution to Western spirituality.[10] I would like to offer reflections on five themes based on the Twelve Steps that develop a spirituality that opens us up to moments of grace in the marketplace: (1) Sharing Our Story, (2) O Happy Fault, (3) Repentance without Regret, (4) Taking an Inventory, and (5) Praying Is Like Eating.

Sharing Our Story. Each of the Twelve Steps begins with the word "we." The human community is made up of broken people. We are all weak. Once we admit this reality then we are on the way to healing. It stands to reason that if we are affected by weakness then our collective structures will also reflect this situation. It dawned on me one day that I am not playing with a full deck of cards, and neither is anyone else around me. What's more, even if we put all of our cards together we still would not have a full deck. There is no such thing as a totally normal person. The term "normal" is relative. Beware of anyone who claims to be normal. There is no such person. That is the human condition. This is the reason for the brokenness and confusion in our world.

Because we are all broken in some way, we are in need of a community where we can share our story. There is hope that comes from the sharing. Often, life is like riding an elevator. We are all having the same experience, but everyone is afraid to talk about it. There is a strength that comes from interacting with one another and sharing our common experiences.

Jesus came not in power but in weakness. He told us that he did not come to be served but to serve. Often, our institutions both ecclesial and political are anything but servant communities. Although many wonderful things came with the conversion of Constantine in 325, an unfortunate effect was the church's acquisition of power. Vestiges of its medieval power structures still remain. To the degree that the church is willing to let go of that power it will experience a collective healing. Then it will be even more fully a place where even the poorest of the poor will be comfortable to come and share their story. Wouldn't it be wonderful if the Statue of Liberty stood in St. Peter's Square inviting the lame, the crippled, and the unwanted to come and seek refuge. The church would then be more fully a home where in the telling of our stories our brokenness would begin to heal.

Regardless of what the institution is ready to do, all of us can begin to create communities wherever we are. I believe that the workplace can become holy if we allow space where people can come to us and share their stories and know that we will accept them in their brokenness. We do not need to create a structure to do this. The way we conduct ourselves, our attitudes, and our way of interacting with others will signal people to come or to keep their distance.

O Happy Fault. My favorite line in the Easter proclamation is "O Happy Fault." These words do not seem to belong together. The fall of humankind, however, would occasion the coming of a messiah, and what a wonderful messiah he turned out to be. Failure can be an opportunity for grace. It can make us aware of our need for a savior. It can make us truly human. Jesus doesn't call us to be successful. He calls us to know our failures and to rely on his power in our lives. We cannot turn over our lives until we recognize our need for a savior.

Fr. Peter, one of my confreres, was always a smashing success. I had gone through high school with him. He got straight A's all through school, was the star athlete, and was the handsomest in our class. After we were ordained, he was the apple of every superior's eye. He got prestigious jobs and always did well. Eventually, he was placed in formation work. He faced one problem after another. The students protested so much that the superiors removed him from office at mid-year. It was a public humiliation for Peter. This was the first time that he had not succeeded. He did not know how to deal with this. He was devastated and eventually went into psychotherapy. After several years, he became a new person. He was much more loving, caring, and compassionate. He was finally human, like the rest of us, knowing that he was weak and needing a savior.

Maybe we all need a crisis point in life before we come to realize this. The pain of crisis can give us the motivation to change. Jesus told us that "anyone who wants to save his life must lose it" (Luke 9:24). Bill Wilson, the founder of Alcoholics Anonymous, puts it this way: "We have to quit playing God."[11] St. Paul understood what it meant to turn over our weaknesses to God:

In view of the extraordinary nature of these revelations, to stop me from getting too proud I was given a thorn in the flesh, an angel of Satan to beat me and stop me from getting too proud. About this thing I pleaded with the Lord three times for it to leave me, but he has said, "My grace is enough for you; my power is at its best in weakness." So I shall be very happy to make my weakness my special boast so that the power of Christ may stay over me, and that is why I am quite content with the weaknesses, insults, hardships, persecutions and the agonies that I go through for Christ's sake, for it is when I am weak that I am strong. (2 Cor. 12:7–10)

This reality is rooted deep within our consciousness as a nation. "In God we trust" is written on all of our money. We need more than our own resources. We need God. I think that in an age of technological development, we need to be reminded that all comes from God. If our individual and collective consciousness would be focused in this way, then our personal lives and corporate existence would be filled with abounding peace and deep-seated righteousness.

Repentance without Regret. It is important to discover where we have gone wrong. We need to name those times and speak them aloud. Again, St. Paul captures this truth in his relationship with the Macedonians. He had to correct them and point out their wrongs:

For even if I saddened you by my letter, I do not regret it....I rejoice now, not because you were saddened, but because you were saddened into repentance; for you were saddened in a godly way, so that you did not suffer loss in anything because of us. For godly sorrow produces a salutary repentance without regret, but worldly sorrow produces death. (2 Cor. 7:9–10)

The review of life and repentance that Alcoholics Anonymous calls people to is not an unhealthy introspection. It is a bidding to take a gentle look at self, see what is really there, and bring it to one another and God for healing. Taking this inventory of one's life can lead to new health. So, too, with our structures. To admit that we have oppressed and excluded people places us on a new path. We know we have wronged others and want to set things straight. So often in our political system we like to bring out the faults in others, not to lead them to new life but rather to crush them. There's a sickness in the way we deal with our leaders. We like to pull them down merely for the sake of destroying them. But God does not want people to wallow in their wrongdoings. We need to know our weaknesses and sins as places from which we grow and come to new life. This is repentance without regret.

A beautiful story about St. Margaret Mary illustrates this point. When Jesus was appearing to her, the parish priest refused to believe Margaret Mary. He told her, "The only way I'll believe these apparitions are happening is if the next time Jesus appears to you he can tell you one of my sins. If you can come back with this information, then I'll believe." After the next apparition, she went back to the priest and said, "Father, I did what you told me when Jesus appeared. When I asked him to tell me one of your sins, he told me to tell you that he doesn't remember any one of them." We should never be afraid to take a moral inventory of our lives. When we point out the faults of our institutions and structures, we should do so firmly but gently because we are inviting the people within them to come to a loving and forgiving God.

Taking an Inventory. It is good to stop and take stock of things in life. We need to take an inventory to know how we're doing. If we don't do this, we will fall into the same pitfalls over and over again.

Affirmations are a good way to begin. Make a list of all the things you would like to be and do, and then write them up as if they are already happening. For example, suppose an area of concern is the lack of physical well-being. Your affirmation would be "I love my body, appreciate it as God's gift, and I like taking care of it." Write a list of affirmations, record them, and listen to them until they sink in. It's the power of positive thinking.

Then think of the shortcomings in your life that you want to change. List the fault and the corresponding positive quality. For example, maybe lying or cheating is a problem for you. List these and then alongside them write "honesty." Again, the focus is not on dwelling on your shortcoming but on a constructive outcome.

Then reflect about the ways your life loses balance. You need to watch these things as warning signals. Possible indicators are poor physical health, tiredness, the absence of a social life or friends, mismanagement of personal finances, etc. List and be aware of those areas that you have a tendency to neglect. Have action plans ready when you find your life going out of balance in the areas you've identified. For example, if you know that you have a tendency to drink too much when you are over-tired, then catch yourself before you get to that point and do something to relax such as going for a long walk in the park or taking a cool swim in the pool.

Then think of the people with whom you need to make amends. Reflect on the ways that you have hurt them and possible ways that you need to be reconciled. Be sure to record your feelings and thoughts about these broken relationships. If there are concrete ways to make amends, then do so. If not, at least pray for the well-being of these people and think of them in a positive, loving, energizing way.

It is important that you take all of this material and share it with another human being in a way that is comfortable for you. The importance of such sharing is clearly rooted in the New Testament. The synoptics include the confession of sins as part of the conversion and baptism called for by John the Baptist (Matt. 3:1–6). When there was a case of some converts who had used occult practices, Acts records that they not only admitted their sins but they had to publicly confess their mistake. "Some came forward to admit in detail how they had used spells. They collected their books and made a bonfire of them in public" (Acts 19:18–19). James the Apostle also advises his penitents, "Confess your sins to one another" (James 5:16). St. John affirms this teaching: "If we acknowledge our sins, then God will forgive our sins" (1 John 1:19). Of course, the story of the Prodigal Son is the most compelling example of taking an inventory of one's life and confessing our findings with another and experiencing the forgiveness and healing that comes from this interaction.

There are many ways of choosing to share our inventory. The most obvious is sharing our story with a trusted friend. If you are fortunate enough to have such a friend, count it a treasure and share your inventory. We are blessed in our culture to have the luxury of therapists and counselors. Certainly, God's healing and freedom can come through their professional background in the therapeutic process. If you come from a religious tradition that has a sacramental system, the sacrament of reconciliation can be a wonderful opportunity for encountering a loving and healing God who offers us strength and courage in facing our sinfulness and addictions. There are also many support groups where you can go and share your story and be affirmed in your journey. Find a way that is helpful for you. What's important is that you take your inventory and find another human being to share where you've been in life and what your hopes are for the future.

Praying Is Like Eating. The steps culminate in prayer and meditation. Regardless of your religious affiliations, it is important that you spend some time with God each day. Again, how you do this is up to you. There is no right or wrong way. It is not my intention here to explain the many forms of prayer. I propose a simple form of reflective meditation. Within each human being there is the healer and the child. The healer wants to free us and the child needs to be guided and cared for. The healer within is what allows the child to become a healthy child. We need to get in touch with the power within us that will heal us.

I propose the following meditation. I suggest that you tape

it and play it back. Sit straight up in a comfortable chair. Fold your hands on your lap and relax. Beginning with your feet and working your way up to your head feel all the tension leaving your body. Spend a few minutes noticing your breathing. Breathe out all that is impure and breathe in all that is good and life-giving.

Picture yourself lying on the beach. Listen to the refreshing sounds of the waves and feel the cool ocean breeze refreshing your face and your entire body. Someone calls you to go for a walk along the ocean. As you walk along you notice a child floating on the waves. You suddenly notice that the child is you at the age of six. The child comes running towards you and you ask the child, "How are you?" How does the child answer? (*listen*).

You and the child go for a long walk along the beach. What do you talk about (*listen*). Then an elderly couple comes and takes you both by the hand up to a large tower overlooking the beach. They tell you that this is the tower of light that enables you to look at your life. The man says, "What's bothering you right now?" (*listen*). The woman says, "What's disturbing you right now?" What do you say?

The man invites you to look at a telescope that envisions the future. You begin to look at your future. How does your child react? It is your choice to put into the future whatever you want. Do it.

The woman tells you that one of the lifeguards just arrived with a gift for you. It is a spiritual gift. Get the gift and open it. What is it?

The man now tells you that you can have any animal you want. Pick an animal that is like you and has special meaning for you. Let the animal be a symbol for you and show you what you need to know.

Walk along the beach with the child. Review what has happened. Tell the child that it is okay to play now, but that you will be back whenever you are needed. You suddenly feel more secure. Rest a little. Enjoy the aftermath of the fantasy and open your eyes slowly, feeling more secure and happy to be alive.

When we think of meditating and praying, we often think we need to go to church. You can do that, but it is not the only way. Pick a spot in your house that can become your "prayer corner." Do something to designate this as sacred space. Maybe place a picture, candle, or a special plant there. Go to that spot and just be there whenever you can. Keep a journal where you write your thoughts and feelings down. You'll be surprised at how it will reveal patterns and directions in your life.

You can make up your own meditations. You can use the Bible. There are many meditation books and tapes available. You can pray and meditate anywhere. For example, riding the train or subway in the morning, notice what you're feeling, the looks on people's faces, and talk to God about this. In your mind wish blessings and peace on the people who accompany you on the train. After you've dropped the kids off at school, spend some time alone thanking God for the day and asking God to help you live it well. At the end of the day, think over the day, what happened, things you're sorry about or happy about. Speak to God about these things. Thank God for the day, both its ups and downs, and ask God's blessing on the next day.

It is important that you make time for solitude and quiet in your life. This is absolutely essential for spiritual growth. However, in the messiness of the marketplace, we might not always be able to have this kind of quiet. This does not mean that we cannot pray. I recall one of the most moving experiences of prayer that I ever had happened in Kennedy Airport. I arrived early for a flight to Europe. The prior days were hectic, filled with last-minute details and work obligations. I finally sat and relaxed in the airport. There were the usual announcements over the loud speakers, with the usual hustling and bustling going on all around me. I sat down, closed my eyes, and started to image Psalm 23: "The Lord is my Shepherd." I pictured the Good Shepherd caring for the sheep. I imagined him picking me up, carrying me in his arms across the ocean. I had never before felt so much peace before a flight. The afterglow of those few minutes of reflective meditation sustained and propelled my spirit to relax and be peaceful as it flew across the Atlantic.

Developing prayerful, meditative habits will make us people who want to share our newfound peace and healing with others. We will want to give it away. People will begin to see a special light in us. They will want it. We should pray so much that we actually become a prayer. The rhythm of our lives will invite other people who want to be healthy and happy to come and be with us. The bottom line is that there is only one way to pray and that is by doing it. Praying is like eating. No one else can do it for you.

Spiritual Blueprints

Becoming more reflective is no small task. Even though we may notionally want to do this, doing it is another question. We need to develop concrete methods to help us focus and actually become reflective. We need to be careful that our introspection gradually moves us beyond ourselves. From a Gospel perspective, all authentic introspection should lead to growth and involvement in life. Anything short of this can be narcissistic. In the past year, two major magazines, *Life* and *Newsweek*, carried cover stories on prayer. *Life* based its story on the premise that in a complex world there are more and more reasons why we pray. The survey revealed that nine out of ten Americans pray frequently and earnestly with a full 51 percent indicating that they pray once or twice a day and 24 percent praying three or more times a day. Ninety-eight percent of the people surveyed said they have prayed for their families, 92 percent for forgiveness, and 23 percent for victory in sports events. Ninety-five percent claimed that they have had the experience of their prayers being answered.[12] Around the same time, *Newsweek* had a cover story entitled, "Talking to God: An Intimate Look at the Way We Pray." The editors wrote, "This week, if you believe at all in opinion surveys, more of us will pray than will go to work or exercise or have sexual relations."

There are many ways that we can open ourselves to God's presence in our lives. Certainly the church offers a variety of opportunities through its liturgy, sacraments, and teachings. The

mystical tradition and the many forms of prayer open up countless avenues for encountering the divine. The universe and the
beauty of nature shout loudly and clearly about the presence
and power of God. There are other ways that are not mentioned
as frequently but are equally grace-filled opportunities for experiencing the transcendent in our lives. I'll treat them under the
following points: (1) Dreams, (2) Spiritual Direction, (3) God's
Face in Beauty, (4) A Vow of Conversation, and (5) The Bible
and the *New York Times*.

Listening to Your Dreams. We spend a substantial portion of
our lives sleeping. During sleep dreams always occur, even
though we often do not remember them. We can learn a lot
about God and ourselves by paying attention to our dreams. We
can begin by noticing our dreams and keeping a dream notebook. This will help us to remember and to observe patterns
over periods of time.

The Scriptures contain many stories about dreams. Jacob's
dream is one of the earliest recorded:

> When he came upon a certain shrine, as the sun had al-
> ready set, he stopped there for the night. Taking one of the
> stones at the shrine, he put it under his head and lay down
> to sleep in that spot. Then he had a dream: a stairway
> rested on the ground, with its top reaching to the heavens;
> and God's messengers were going up and down it. (Gen.
> 28:11–12).

Joseph is another example of one who dreams in the Hebrew Scriptures. He was even called a dreamer by his brothers.
It was his gift of interpreting dreams that endeared him to the
pharaoh. As a result, he became a powerful figure in Egypt and
was able to use his position to bring freedom to his family.

The New Testament dreamer is St. Joseph. It was in a dream
that the angel spoke to him and told him to flee with Mary and
Jesus to Egypt. Maybe St. Joseph should be the patron of dream
analysis.

The fact that God communicates in dreams is clearly stated

in the book of Job. "For God does speak, perhaps once, or even twice, though one perceives it not. In a dream, in a vision of the night, when deep sleep falls upon people, as they slumber in their beds. It is then that God opens the ears of people" (Job 33:14–15). If dreams are another way that we can encounter the mystery of God, then we should learn to interpret and understand them.

Dream experts tell us that 90 percent of the content and persons in dreams reflect the dreamer and the dreamer's concerns. Freud taught that dreams were the royal road to the unconscious. Jung believed that dreams were manifestations about the deepest realities of life. Dreams often reveal something about our past that has not been resolved, give an insight into a present situation, or can even predict the future. Dreams can certainly enhance the spiritual journey by elucidating and integrating elements of our conscious and unconscious lives.

There are two types of dreams, "day dreams" and "this is my life dreams." Day dreams are related to a current event in your life. For example, just last night I had a dream about this book. I dreamt about the color of the cover and an unfinished chapter. I was anxious in the dream and woke up with that feeling. The dream underscored my concern about finishing this last chapter and getting it out to the publisher on time. "This is my life" dreams tell us about unresolved life issues. Frequently, these kinds of dreams are recurring and are themes that we share with others. For example, I often dream about my father. In these dreams we usually are conversing about what's happening in the world. The dream often ends with a kiss or embrace. Since my father died during my adolescence, I never had the opportunity to develop an adult relationship with him. That's what is now happening in these dreams. It helps to give dreams of this type a title that will easily bring them to memory and can become material for prayer or reflection. I group the dreams about my father under the title, "Mr. Dad."

Paying attention to dreams should lead to action in our lives. Honor them by listening to God's communication and by responding with a 'definite course of action, for example, resolving hurts, completing unfinished current agenda, or planning for the future. St. Joseph acted on his dream by fleeing into Egypt. This tradition goes back to the book of Samuel, who heard the Lord calling him in his dreams. At first Samuel was unfamiliar with God's communication through dreams. "Samuel was not familiar with the Lord, because the Lord had not revealed anything to him yet" (1 Sam. 3:7). When he finally understood that it was Yahweh calling him in his dream, he responded: "Here I am Lord, your servant is listening" (1 Sam. 8–9). Once he knew it was the Lord, he was not afraid to act on what God was telling him to do.[13]

Spiritual Direction. In becoming more aware of self, God, and others in the experiences of daily life, some kind of spiritual direction can be of great value. My interpretation of spiritual direction is broad-based. People mean a lot of different things by the term.

First of all, let's look at what it is not. Spiritual direction is not counseling or psychotherapy. Counseling usually focuses on particular problems or issues in one's life, while therapy is concerned with developmental problems or personality disorders. These avenues can be very helpful to us at different times in our lives, but they are not spiritual direction.

Spiritual direction is not one person telling another what to do. It is not some esoteric experience in which one person has some special knowledge. Be very careful of people who claim that they know God's will for you. Nobody has the inside corner on God's will. God's will is not a thing that can be mediated in such a simplistic way. Often God's will manifests itself over a long period of time and frequently is not very direct. God often gives us several paths that we might follow. There is no such thing as spiritual direction that dictates God's will to you.

Spiritual direction is not problem-oriented. It does not involve a person going to a spiritual director with a list of problems to be solved. This does not mean that problems that arise cannot be included in spiritual direction. But the essence of spiritual direction should not be the resolution of problems.

In the past, many people thought that going to confession was spiritual direction. The purpose of the sacrament of reconciliation is not to give spiritual direction. Its purpose is to pray and offer God's healing through the forgiveness of sins. The words offered by the minister in this sacrament are usually words of encouragement to live the Christian life and to continue on the spiritual journey.

If spiritual direction is not any of these things, what is it? I propose that spiritual direction is simply facilitating a person's relationship with God. The director listens to the directee describe what's happening in the relationship. The goal is to keep the directee in relationship with God and to help him or her to develop the relationship and move it to the next step.

Discernment is often an issue within the spiritual direction process. In my definition of spiritual direction, discernment's goal should be whatever is best going to keep a person in relationship with God. This is the vantage point from which all decisions should be made.

Given all these qualifications, I think that spiritual direction means different things to people at different moments in their lives. For example, at the beginning of a spiritual journey that involves a conversion from a life of sin, spiritual direction might be rather frequent and last for a long period of time. When decisions need to be made about life choices like marriage, priesthood, or religious life, spiritual direction may last for the period in which the decision is being made. People might move in and out of spiritual direction at different times in their lives.

Generally, I would say that each session should last for about one hour. In the beginning stages, meetings should be more frequent, simply to develop the relationship between the director and directee. Once that has happened, director and directee should agree on the frequency of meetings. For some, it might be monthly or every six weeks. Some people like to meet several times a year and schedule these times according to the change in seasons.

In addition to formal spiritual direction sessions, I also believe that direction can happen in other ways. In the Eastern church, a spiritual director is called a soul friend. A solid friendship that focuses on God, one in which people are free to talk about their inner spirits and their ups and downs, can be a form of spiritual direction. These kinds of relationships were often experienced by the saints. For example, St. Francis and St. Clare had such a relationship. In making important decisions about future directions in his life, St. Francis would often pray and confer with St. Clare.

Direction can also happen in a group context. For example, some Bible study or prayer groups reach a degree of intimacy and trust where people can share quite openly their journey with the Lord. Some support groups can also serve this purpose. I help coordinate an AIDS support group in which participants share their hurts and fears and questions in the context of their relationship with God. In this informal atmosphere, I have witnessed solid spiritual direction given and received.

Spiritual direction can also happen within the liturgy. Recently, a young doctor came to see me. He told me that for several years he has been praying with the lectionary each day. He would also go to the Eucharist daily where he knew an excellent homily based on the Scriptures would be given. He lived his life and developed a relationship with God around the readings and homilies. The liturgy became an experience of spiritual direction for him.

The form that spiritual direction takes for you will depend on your needs and sensitivities. What's important and critical to remember is that growth along the spiritual path doesn't happen without effort. Any kind of growth, whether spiritual, intellectual, or physical, requires some initiative on our part as well as some guidance and direction. The tools and the tradition of spiritual direction have a great deal to offer anyone who is serious about experiencing the transcendent in everyday life.

God's Face in Beauty. Another way of becoming more reflective in the marketplace is by taking the time to pay attention to the beauty that surrounds us. The mystic is one who can find beauty in the midst of the ordinary. I often think of this when I look at still-life paintings. I am always moved by the deep sensitivity of the artist who can pay attention to what most of us take for granted. Marcel Proust wrote that the still-life paintings of Jean Baptiste Siméon Chardin revived the senses to portray the mystery of ordinary things:

> If, when looking at Chardin, you can say to yourself, "This is intimate, this is comfortable, this is as living as a kitchen," then, when you are walking around a kitchen, you will say to yourself, "This is special, this is great, this is as beautiful as a Chardin." Chardin may have been merely a man who enjoyed his dining-room, among the fruits and glasses, but he was also a man with a sharper awareness, whose pleasure was so intense that it overflowed into smooth strokes, eternal colors. You, too, will be a Chardin, not so great, perhaps, but great to the extent that you love him, identify yourself with him, become like him, a person for whom metal and stoneware are living and to whom fruit speaks.[14]

It is this kind of awareness that will see the divine in the ordinary. Cultivating an appreciation of beauty is a door to the sacred. Reading a poem, going to a Broadway play, or walking through a museum can be sacramental events. In an age of computers and machines, it is more critical than ever that we develop the intuitive components of our personalities. The arts provide a wonderful opportunity for nurturing the sensitive, instinctive, and passionate within us.

Art invites interaction. It reveals beauty, life, and a message. Often the meaning of art cannot be captured in words but can only be felt. True art cannot be talked about. It has to be experienced. Good art succeeds in capturing the transcendent in a fleeting moment in time. For example, Beethoven's Ninth Symphony was such a moment. He felt that all that he ever wanted to communicate was given in this piece of music. It is very much like the hand of the human person reaching up to touch the hand of God in Michelangelo's beautiful fresco in the Sistine Chapel.

Art reveals something of God. The pain, the joys, the confusion, and the wonder of life are captured in colors, verses, notes, and stories. Art points beyond itself. Art makes emotions come alive. There is a wisdom in preaching God's word through art. I think we convince people of doctrine more by singing and dancing than by pointing fingers and issuing threats.

Art keeps memory alive and reinforces the values that we hold most dear. True art challenges us by pulling us into a tradition and then forging us beyond it. In some ways, art is the greatest tool we have for conveying God's message in everyday life. I think that it was this awareness about art's power that inspired the Council Fathers at the end of the Second Vatican Council to address all the artists of the world:

> We now address you, artists, who are taken up with beauty and work for it: poets and literary men, painters, sculptors, architects, musicians, men devoted to the theater and the cinema. To all of you, the church of the council declares to you through our voice: if you are friends of genuine art, you are our friends. This world in which we live needs beauty in order not to sink into despair. It is beauty, like truth, which brings joy to the hearts of man and is that precious fruit which resists the wear and tear of time, which unites generations and makes them share things in admiration. And all of this is through your hands. May these hands be pure and disinterested. Remember that you are the guardians of beauty in the world.[15]

I do not think it is a small accident that the council included an address to artists. As the "guardians of beauty," their role is a critical one in today's society. I would suggest that we are all called to be artists, to perceive the divine in the midst of the ordinary. The ways in which we develop this artistic sense will vary among us. It is important that we experience art each day in some way. Beauty is all around us if only we would stop and notice. Besides the small events of every day, we should read a novel every now and then, go to a good movie or to the theater or opera, have a nicely prepared meal, and listen to some good music. And most of all, "Enjoy!" and let that enjoyment rest in your heart. Give it away to the next person you meet. Then all of life will be art.

A Vow of Conversation. As we talk with others about our dreams, the beauty of art, and the events in the news, we have another opportunity to touch the transcendent. Thomas Merton once wrote that he would take a vow of conversation. That seems like a strange statement from someone in a community that at one time was so protective of silence that members used sign language. I often think of a story I once heard about a Trappist monastery. While the monks were asleep, the monastery caught fire. The symbol in sign language for fire is the placing of the index finger over the lips. A monk awakened during the fire. Being obedient and valuing the monastic silence, he raced down the corridors, not shouting, but with his finger over his lips. Fortunately, he slipped and knocked over a bookcase. The monks were awakened by the noise, and their lives were saved.

Giving the rigidity of the context in which an event like this supposedly happened, it is truly amazing that the word "conversation" would even occur to a monk. A closer look at the etymology of the word "conversation" reveals a deep level of meaning. In its Latin root, the word means "to keep company with" and "to turn around." To live in the company of other human beings means to pay attention, to take their presence seriously, and to look at any encounter with another as sacred. In genuine encounters of this type, there is the potential to turn around ideas, viewpoints, and prejudices. It is not a violent process but rather one where change comes about in the spark of quality interaction between two human beings.

Merton's vow of conversation was one in which he looked at the world and the people who came his way as opportunities for growth. The Emmaus story is an excellent paradigm for this kind of holy conversation:

Two of them that same day were making their way to
a village named Emmaus seven miles distant from Jerusalem, discussing as they went all that had happened. In
the course of their lively exchange, Jesus approached and
began to walk along with them. However, they were re-
frained from recognizing him. He said to them, "What are
you discussing as you go your way?" They halted, in distress, and one of them, Cleopas by name, asked him, "Are
you the only resident of Jerusalem who does not know
the things that went on there these past few days?" (Luke
24:13–18)

Initially, the disciples were so engrossed in idle "chit-chat" that
they were incapable of welcoming a guest. Their agenda was
too packed to be open to this person who happened to walk
into their lives.

This is how we so often live. God is often in the intermis-
sions of life that are unplanned, where nothing seems to be
happening. I think God is more in the accidents of life than in
the programs we have prepared. By inviting the unexpected and
welcoming strangers with reverence, there is the opportunity for
conversation to occur. Often in the Hebrew Scriptures, to welcome a guest was to entertain an angel. Angels continue to walk
among us. Each time we open our hearts to the unexpected
and offer conversation and companionship we are entertaining
sacred guests.

As we live and go about the tasks of everyday life, it would
be a tragedy never to allow unexpected conversation to occur.
Such conversation can be exciting and growth-producing for the
human spirit. Fortunately, the disciples finally welcomed their
guest and in the act of conversation recognized, "Were not our
hearts burning inside us as he conversed with us on the road?"
(Luke 24:32). True conversation places passion in our hearts,
visions in our minds, and wind at our feet. Live life expecting
conversation to happen not only in your intimate relationships,
but also at moments, in places, and with people whom you least
expect. Wouldn't it be great if at life's end we could look back

and say "Weren't our hearts burning as we conversed along the way?"

The Bible and the New York Times. As disciples in the marketplace, we are called to have conversation not only with individuals but with the whole world as its events unfold in the daily news. Karl Barth once suggested that every preacher should hold a Bible in one hand and the *New York Times* in the other. I would extend Barth's statement to include not only preachers but all men and women living in today's world. Reading the newspaper is holy time. A priest who recently came for spiritual direction was talking about prayer. He felt guilty because the first thing he does in the morning is read the newspapers. Then he spends some time in formal prayer.

Reading the paper can be a way of praying. The newspaper puts us in touch with the larger world and its concerns. It forces us to move beyond the narrow worldview of our parochialism and our own personal needs. It is the world that God passionately embraces. I was recently visiting a nursing home for retired religious. What struck me as I went through many of the bedrooms was that so many of them had either statues or pictures of the Sacred Heart. I felt kind of foolish when I made note of this to the superior, and she told me the reason for this was that the name of their community is the "Apostles of the Sacred Heart." I hadn't thought about this particular devotion for many years. I was suddenly touched by the emphasis on the heart in the pictures and statues. I also noted that in almost all of the images Jesus' arms were outstretched.

This is a great image for reading the newspapers. Read the papers with your heart and with outstretched arms. Welcome the people you read about into your life. Take the needs of the world into your prayer. Make the concerns of the world your concerns. If it is possible in any way to take some concrete action, such as a letter to your congressional representative, your senator, or the newspaper editor, then do it. Or maybe you could make a donation of money, food, or clothing in response to a tragedy in your community. It is hard to imagine going to pray without bringing what you read in the newspaper with you. Prayer is not a peaceful escape from life. On the contrary, it is a challenge to get more deeply involved in the world around you. Reflective prayer changes every day because the newspaper changes daily. Thus, the focus of our prayer must change to embrace the world as we find it when we wake up in the morning.

Conclusion

Living in the marketplace invites a spirituality that is practical and focused on the world as it truly is from nine to five. Jesus has shown us how to become holy by being human and concerned about the needs of all. As Americans, it is imperative that we become holy within this culture and enhance those American values that are compatible with the Gospel. At the same time, everyday mystics should help transform into something positive those negative values and trends within the culture that are contrary to the Gospel.

To become this kind of mystic means that we must pay attention and become aware of the energies within and around us. It doesn't matter whether Alcoholics Anonymous, dreams, spiritual direction, art, conversation, or the daily newspaper help you to do this. What matters is that you choose specific ways that will help you to grow and become more reflective. An old Peruvian proverb says it well:

> Pilgrim, pilgrim, pilgrim
> There is no way, there is no way, there is no way.
> You make the way, you make the way, you make the way,
> By walking, walking, walking.

Reflection Starters

1. Who is your Jesus? Draw a picture of what he looks like or write a description. How does your image of Jesus have an impact on the way you live?

2. Make an inventory of your life as prescribed by Alcoholics Anonymous. Then go for a walk or dinner with a friend and share as much of it as you can.

3. Pay attention to your dreams for one week. Keep a notebook alongside your bed. Upon awaking, record your dreams. At the end of the week, review your dreams and notice any patterns or themes.

4. Go to an art museum. Absorb and breathe in the beauty. Then go for a long walk, live in the afterglow of the experience, and then do something to bring that feeling of beauty into the life of another person.

Conclusion

Saint, n. *A dead sinner revised and edited.*
— AMBROSE BIERCE, *The Devil's Dictionary*

I recently read the story of a former Trappist abbot who is now a hermit. He was asked by a group of Trappistine nuns to be their chaplain. His community did not want him to go. They said, "We need our hermit on the hill, joyously in love with God for its own sake. Otherwise we will forget why we are doing what we are doing." As we live everyday life it is essential to remember why we are here. Yes, we have tasks to perform and duties to fulfill. From God's eyes, we are here to do these things with love for God and one another. To forget that would be to make our everyday lives dull and meaningless.

A way of achieving this end is to do our best to live each day as God gives it to us, not as we would like it to be. Brother Lawrence, a simple lay brother of the eighteenth century, developed a spirituality called the "Practice of the Presence of God."[1] There is nothing complicated about his insight. He simply suggests that we do our best to be aware of God's presence in the midst of our daily lives.

Jean Pierre de Caussade, writing in the early part of the eighteenth century, developed Brother Lawrence's idea. Caussade coined the phrase "the Sacrament of the Present Moment."[2] His spirituality was to accept the state in which we find ourselves as the one God wishes for us. To be rooted and attentive to where we are in this moment is the key to holiness.

In our own time, Zen Buddhists have made a wonderful con-

178

tribution in their emphasis on just being in the present moment. Having experienced numerous meditation sessions practicing just being in the now, I can testify how difficult it is for us who live life in the fast lane to put everything aside to live completely focused on the present moment.

I do not mean to suggest that we abandon the past. Often there is material from our past that we need to work through in order to lead fuller lives. Also it is important to be nourished by the memories of our traditions. We would also be foolish and irresponsible not to plan for the future. However, all should be done from our rootedness in the present moment. We need to remember that the God who clothes the lilies of the field and the birds of the air has counted even the hairs of our head. No need to worry. Emmanuel, God is with us, in the here and now.

We need to practice the presence of God. Even if for just five minutes each day, we need to block everything out of our minds and simply be in the presence of God. I believe that this would give us the strength to move through the day filled with hope and courage. Otherwise, we run on our own short-lived steam.

This way of living is eucharistic. When Christians celebrate Eucharist, they remember and tell their stories from the past. In this event, they experience the presence of the Risen Christ in the marketplace, with their eyes fixed to a glorious future when Christ will come again in the fullness of time. The liturgy of Eucharist has little if any meaning if Eucharist is not happening in everyday life. In this sense, we become sacraments for one another, holy moments for discovering God in one another's eyes.

Several years ago I was giving retreats in Louisiana. One day the married couples sponsoring the retreats invited me to go with them to a little town called Carville, where the only leprosarium in North America is located.[3] The complex is quite large, housing about one thousand people. As they brought me around to meet some of the people, I couldn't help but notice their joyful spirits.

When we went into the chapel, there was a beautiful woman in the first row. Her name was Maria. She was praying. When she heard us coming in, she very graciously got up from her prayer and came to greet us. I later found out that Maria was from Latin America and had contracted leprosy as a young girl. Sent by her parents to the leprosarium, she has been there for over twenty years.

She took us into a little dining area and served us tea. She had many questions about who I was and what I do. She was genuinely interested in each of us and conveyed a warm and gentle hospitality. Maria was truly inspiring. We spent a wonderful hour with her. As we were driving away, I noticed that she was going back into the chapel. The couples said, "We wanted you to meet her. We think Maria is a saint. If she's not in the chapel, she's out helping the others. She always greets us with a smile. We never feel that we are intruding in her life."

I agree with my friends. I think Maria is a holy woman. She is a mystic in everyday life. Her prayer in the chapel led her to embrace us with kindness and her conversation with us led her back to the chapel. This is the mystical rhythm, going from prayer to life and back to prayer. Maria was a mystic living Eucharist, embracing the body of Christ in us, practicing the presence of God in everyday life.

God is the God of the now. In the Hebrew Scriptures God is named "I Am." When we get caught in the past and bogged down with our guilt we are worshiping the God who was. When we become obsessed about tomorrow and its needs, we are worshiping the God who will be. Both of these are false gods. God's name is not I was or I will be. God's name is I AM.

Notes

Introduction

1. The Second Vatican Council was called by Pope John XXIII and was held from 1962 to 1965. The purpose of the council was to update and renew the church so that it might more fully respond to the changing needs of the modern world.

2. Dogmatic Constitution on the Church, 39–40, in Austin Flannery, O.P., ed., *Vatican Council II: The Conciliar and Post Conciliar Documents* (Grand Rapids Mich.: William B. Eerdmans Publishing Co., 1992).

3. Dogmatic Constitution on the Church, 8.

4. The Cappadocian Fathers lived and wrote in the fourth century. The Greek Fathers developed the monastic tradition to include the movement of the human person in a gradual process toward union with God.

5. For a complete explanation of Rahner's theology of mysticism, see Karl Rahner, *Theological Investigations*, vol. 3, *Theology of the Spiritual Life* (Baltimore and London: Helicon Press, 1967).

6. Dag Hammarskjold, *Markings* (New York: Knopf, 1965), 89.

Chapter One: Wisdom on Wall Street

1. When I use the term "Wall Street" throughout this text, I am writing on two levels. The first meaning is the New York financial district. The second meaning is everyday life, where and how you live life each day. This will mean different things for different people. It can even vary from day to day. For example, life from nine to five can be lived at work, home, school, or simply can be leisure or recreation time.

2. I did my dissertation on liberation theology. This particular method of doing theology was developed in Latin America. It challenges the political, ecclesial, and economic systems that oppress people and

deprive them of their dignity. The irony is that I was writing this dissertation on Wall Street, which is the center of the American capitalistic system, which played no small part in the economic oppression of Third World countries.

3. John Paul II, *Sollicitudo Rei Socialis* in *Origins* 17, no. 38 (March 3, 1988). In this encyclical Pope John Paul commemorates the twentieth anniversary of Pope Paul VI's social encyclical *Populorum Progressio*. In this very challenging piece Pope John Paul calls for an interdependence among all nations and a more equitable sharing of the world's resources. He addresses the economic structures of both the East and West.

4. Oscar Wilde, *A Woman of No Importance* (Boston: Wyman-Fogg Co., 1909), 3.

5. Bernard Lonergan, *Method in Theology* (New York: Seabury Press, 1972). In this work, Lonergan not only explains conversion but also presents an excellent way for studying theology.

6. J. D. Salinger, *Franny and Zooey* (Boston: Little Brown, 1961).

7. By voices I mean the inner stirrings within a human person. These stirrings include the feelings, moods, and drives that everyone experiences. Unconscious manifestations include dreams, fantasies, and random wanderings of the mind.

8. St. Ignatius developed this method during a hospital stay after being injured in a battle. He experienced a conversion by paying attention to what he was feeling. By doing this, he began to realize that sensations that gave him immediate gratification did not sustain him for a long period. On the other hand, when reading the Scriptures and the lives of the saints, he noticed that there was a long-lasting peace that followed from responding to these urges. This process was the beginning of his famous rules for the discernment of spirits. These are explained in his spiritual exercises: Louis J. Puhl, S.J., trans., *The Spiritual Exercises of St. Ignatius* (Westminster, Md.: Newman Press, 1960).

9. For a detailed study of various personality theories and systems of psychotherapies see Raymond Corsini, ed., *Current Psychotherapies* (Itasca, Ill.: F. E. Peacock Publishers, 1973). This is not to equate spirituality with psychology. Since both disciplines are concerned about the workings of the human spirit, it is helpful to review elements that are supportive of each other.

10. Pelagianism was a heresy in the early centuries of the church that emphasized that we must earn our salvation by what we do. This particular heresy is especially attractive to us Americans, who are rooted in a Puritan work ethic. The opposite of Pelagianism is the belief that our actions begin by God's initiative.

11. For a thorough study of St. Teresa's spirituality, see E. Allison

Peers, ed., *The Complete Works of St. Teresa of Jesus* (New York: Sheed and Ward, 1972).

12. An excellent work for researching primary sources on the writings and early biographies of St. Francis is Marion A. Habig, ed., *St. Francis of Assisi: Writings and Early Biographies* (Chicago: Franciscan Herald Press, 1972). For the story about the breaking of the fast, see Thomas of Celano, *The Second Life of St. Francis,* chapters 14 and 15, 374–75.

13. St. Augustine, *Confessions,* trans. Henry Chadwick (New York: Oxford University Press, 1991), 3.

14. Our age is in many ways an apocalyptic one. One indicator of this is the current interest in the book of Revelation. Many people incorrectly interpret this book and its symbols to prove that we are living in the last days. The crumbling social, religious, and economic structures of our day lend themselves to this apocalyptic mood. For an excellent study of apocalypticism, see Bernard McGinn, trans., *Apocalyptic Spirituality,* Classics of Western Spirituality (New York: Paulist Press, 1979).

15. *Hamlet,* 1.3.68.

Chapter Two: Dangerous Dreams and Rude Awakenings

1. Dag Hammarskjold, *Markings* (New York: Knopf, 1965), 205.

2. Bonaventure, *The Soul's Journey into God,* ed. Ewert Cousins (New York: Paulist Press, 1978). In this excellent volume, Cousins situates *The Soul's Journey into God* with St. Bonaventure's other two spiritual works, *The Tree of Life* and *The Life of St. Francis.* It is important to read the trilogy. The spirituality of *The Soul's Journey* is concretely illustrated in the other two works.

3. An excellent presentation of the spirituality of the life stages can be found in Evelyn and James Whitehead, *Christian Life Patterns* (New York: Doubleday, 1979).

4. For a detailed explanation of the early stages of development, see Erik Erikson, *Childhood and Society* (New York: W. W. Norton & Company, 1956). Erikson's work is classic for understanding the developmental process. For a detailed study on the impact of the family on human development, see John Bradshaw, *The Family* (Deerfield Beach, Fla.: Health Communications, 1988).

5. James Fowler, *Stages of Faith: The Psychology of Human Development and the Quest for Meaning* (San Francisco: Harper and Row, 1981); James Fowler, *Weaving the New Creation: Stages of Faith and the Public Church* (San Francisco: Harper and Row, 1991).

6. Daniel J. Levinson, *The Seasons of a Man's Life* (New York: Knopf, 1978), is an excellent volume for appreciating the tasks and challenges of adult development.

7. See Joanne Sabol Stevenson, *Issues and Crises during Middlescence* (New York: Appleton-Century-Crofts, 1977), and Anne Brennan and Janice Brewi, *Mid-Life Directions* (New York: Paulist Press, 1985). Both are good works for explaining the issues of mid-life.

8. See Eugene C. Bianchi, *Aging as a Spiritual Journey* (New York: Crossroad, 1982), a beautiful work on the spirituality of old age.

9. Claude Cuenot, *Teilhard de Chardin* (Baltimore: Helicon, 1965).

10. Thornton Wilder, *The Skin of Our Teeth,* act 2.

11. George Orwell, "Reflections on Gandhi," in *Shooting an Elephant* (1950).

12. See Daniel J. Levinson, *The Seasons of a Man's Life* (New York: Knopf, 1978). Levinson was one of the first to write about adult development and the readjustment of ideals. A serious shortcoming of his study is that he looks at these issues only from a masculine perspective. For a good work explaining the developmental process from a feminine experience, see Catherine Bateson, *Composing a Life* (New York: New American Library, 1989).

13. Thomas Merton, *Mystics and Zen Masters* (New York: Delta Books, 1967), 12.

14. Thomas Merton, *The Seven Storey Mountain* (New York: Harcourt, Brace and Company, 1948), 28–29.

15. Thomas Merton, *Conjectures of a Guilty Bystander* (New York: Image Books, 1968), 149.

16. *Cistercian Studies* 23, no. 4 (1978): 395.

17. Naomi Burton, Patrick Hart, and James Laughlin, eds., *The Asian Journal of Thomas Merton* (New York: New Directions, 1973), 233.

18. Ibid., 379.

19. Thomas Merton, *Thoughts in Solitude* (New York: Farrar, Straus and Cudahy, 1958), 32.

Chapter Three: Writing Straight with Crooked Lines

1. For further reading on Jansenism, see Blaise Pascal, *Pensées,* trans. A. J. Krailsheimer (Baltimore: Penguin Books, 1966); Hans Urs von Balthasar, *The Glory of the Lord* (San Francisco: Ignatius Press, 1986), 3:172–238.

2. "The Martyrdom of Saint Polycarp," in *The Acts of the Christian Martyrs,* trans. and introduced by H. Musurillo (New York: Oxford, 1972), 1922–93.

3. Louis Bouyer, *The Spirituality of the New Testament and the Fathers* (New York: Seabury Press, 1982), 203.

4. For a good summary of Origen's teachings, see Johannes Quasten,

Patrology, vol. 2, Christian Classics (Philadelphia: Westminster, 1983), 37–101.

5. Margaret R. Miles, "The Recovery of Asceticism," *Commonweal,* January 28, 1943, 40–43.

6. "The Letter of the Church of Lyons and Vienne," in *The Acts of the Christian Martyrs,* 79–81. The letter is preserved in Eusebius's *Ecclesiastical History,* Book V.

7. Jules M. Brady, ed., *An Augustine Treasury* (Boston: Daughters of St. Paul, 1981).

8. E. Allison Peers, ed., *The Complete Works of St. Teresa of Jesus* (New York: Sheed and Ward, 1972).

9. For a complete study of the social teachings of the church since Pope John XXIII, see Joseph Gremillion, ed., *The Gospel of Peace and Justice* (Maryknoll, N.Y.: Orbis Books, 1976); Judith A. Dwyer, ed. *The New Dictionary of Catholic Social Thought* (Collegeville, Minn.: Liturgical Press, 1994); John Coleman, ed., *One Hundred Years of Catholic Social Thought* (Maryknoll, N.Y.: Orbis Books, 1991)

10. Arnold Fortini, *Francis of Assisi,* translation of *Nova Vita di San Francesco,* trans. Helen Moak (New York: Crossroad, 1981), 208–10.

11. "The Life of St. Francis," in Ewert Cousins, ed., *Bonaventure* (New York: Paulist Press, 1978), 188–89.

Chapter Four: A Spirituality of Collaboration

1. Roland E. Murphy, "Canticle of Canticles," in Raymond Brown et al., eds., *The Jerome Biblical Commentary* (Englewood Cliffs, N.J.: Prentice Hall, 1968), 506–10.

2. A few books that might be helpful in reflecting on sexuality: Joan H. Timmerman, *Sexuality and Spiritual Growth* (New York: Crossroad, 1992); Thomas Tyrrell, *Urgent Longing: Reflections on the Experience of Infatuation, Human Intimacy, and Contemplative Love* (Whitinsville, Mass.: Affirmation Books, 1980); Robert T. Francoeur, *Becoming a Sexual Person* (New York: John Wiley, 1984).

3. For further reflections about anger, see Brendan P. Riordan, ed., *Anger* (Whitinsville, Mass.: Affirmation Books, 1985); Carol Tavaris, *Anger: The Misunderstood Emotion* (New York: Simon and Schuster, 1982); Andrew D. Lester, *Coping with Your Anger* (Philadelphia: Westminster Press, 1983).

4. Feodor Dostoyevsky, "Critical Articles: Introduction," *Polnoye Sobraniye Sochinyeni* (*Complete Collected Works,* 1895), v. 9.

5. For an excellent comparison between St. Thomas Aquinas and St. Bonaventure, see Robert W. Shahan and Francis J. Kovach, eds.,

Bonaventure and Aquinas (Norman: University of Oklahoma Press, 1976).

6. See Robert N. Bellah et al., *Habits of the Heart* (New York: Harper and Row, 1985), viii.

7. See Caietanus Esser, O.F.M., ed., *Opuscula Sancti Patris Francisci Assisiensis* (Rome: Grotta Ferrata, 1978), 86–88. The text is a free translation by the author of "The Canticle of Brother Sun."

8. Prayer written by Charles K. Robinson, distributed by Damien Ministries, Washington, D.C.

9. Elbert Hubbard, *The Note Book,* 1927.

Chapter Five: Cunning as Serpents, Gentle as Doves

1. Nicholai de Cusa, *Opera Omnia,* vol. 1, *De Docta Ignorantia,* ed. E. Hoffmann and R. Klibansky, 1932; ET: Nicholas of Cusa, *The Vision of God* (Hamburg: Meiner, 1960).

2. Ewert H. Cousins, *Bonaventure and the Coincidence of Opposites* (Chicago: Franciscan Herald Press, 1977). Cousins presents an excellent study on the foundations of the coincidence of opposites and its application to twentieth-century thought.

3. The church in Latin America is a poignant example of this. For centuries the hierarchy affiliated itself with the power structures that were oppressive to the poor. Fortunately, in recent years in response to papal social teachings and the work of liberation theologians, many in the Latin American church increasingly are opting for the poor.

4. H. Richard Niebuhr, *Christ and Culture* (New York: Harper Torchbooks, 1951).

5. Erma Bombeck, *Aunt Erma's Cope Book* (New York: Fawcett Crest, 1979), 47–53.

6. Robert Anderson, *Stress Power: How to Turn Your Tension into Energy* (New York: Human Science Press, 1978), 18.

7. Marion A. Habig, ed., "Sacrum Commercium or Francis and His Lady Poverty," in *St. Francis of Assisi: Writing and Early Biographies* (Chicago: Franciscan Herald Press, 1972), 1531–96.

8. Anthony De Mello, S.J., *The Song of the Bird* (Anand, India: Gujarat Sahitya Prakash, 1982), 114–15.

9. Bernard J. F. Lonergan, *A Second Collection* (Philadelphia: Westminster Press, 1974), 97. Lonergan points out that most saints were not theologians and most theologians were not saints.

10. *The Merchant of Venice,* act 4, sc. 1.

11. Cited in William Barclay, *The Gospel of Matthew* (Philadelphia: Westminster Press, 1956), 109.

12. Rev. James C. Sharp, ed., *Lead Kindly Light* (New York: Catholic Book Publishing Co., 1993), 190.

Chapter Six: Mystics in the Marketplace

1. Thomas N. Hart, *To Know and Follow Jesus* (New York: Paulist Press, 1984), 146.

2. Nikos Kazantzakis, *The Last Temptation of Christ* (New York: Simon and Schuster, 1960), 1.

3. Author unknown.

4. Charles H. Bayer, *A Guide to Liberation Theology for Middle-Class Congregations* (St. Louis, Mo.. CBP Press, 1986), 23.

5. Ibid., 52.

6. Pastoral Constitution on the Church in the Modern World, 1, in Austin Flannery, O.P., ed. *Documents of Vatican II* (New York: Costello, 1984).

7. The notion of wonder is the beginning of the rational process that leads to theological investigation and study. The method begins with the intellectual construct of wonder and proceeds to construct a theological explanation for divine truths.

8. Juan Luis Segundo, *The Liberation of Theology* (Maryknoll, N.Y.: Orbis Books, 1976), 9.

9. Leonardo Boff and Clodovis Boff, *Introducing Liberation Theology*, (Maryknoll, N.Y.: Orbis Books, 1987), 22–43.

10. The actual Twelve Step program is as follows: Step One: We admitted we were powerless over alcohol — that our lives had become unmanageable. Step Two: Came to believe that a Power greater than ourselves could restore us to sanity. Step Three: Made a decision to turn our will and our lives over to the care of God as we understand Him. Step Four: Made a searching and fearless inventory of ourselves. Step Five: Admitted to God, to ourselves, and to another human being the exact nature of our wrongs. Step Six: Were entirely ready to have God remove all these defects of character. Step Seven: Humbly ask Him to remove our shortcomings. Step Eight: Made a list of all persons we had harmed, and became willing to make amends to them all. Step Nine: Made direct amends to such people wherever possible, except when to do so would injure them or others. Step Ten: Continued to take personal inventory and when we were wrong promptly admitted it. Step Eleven: Sought through prayer and meditation to improve our conscious contract with God as we understand him, praying only for knowledge of His will for us and the power to carry that out. Step Twelve: Having had a spiritual awakening as a result of these steps, we tried to carry this message to alcoholics, and to practice these principles in our affairs (*Twelve*

Steps and Twelve Traditions [New York: Alcoholics Anonymous World Services, 1965]). The Twelve Steps are reprinted with permission of Alcoholics Anonymous World Services, Inc. Permission to reprint this material does not mean that A.A. has reviewed or approved the contents of this publication, nor that A.A. agrees with the views expressed herein. A.A. is a program of recovery for alcoholics *only.* Use of the Twelve Steps in connection with programs and activities that are patterned after A.A. but that address other problems does not imply otherwise.

11. *Twelve Steps and Twelve Traditions,* 62.

12. *Life,* March 1994, 54–82.

13. See Robert S. Clark, F.M.S., "Dreams and the Spiritual Journey," from a workshop given at Convocation '94 at the College of St. Elizabeth, Morristown, N.J. Also see Ellan Freeman Sharpe, *Dream Analysis: A Practical Approach* (New York: Brunner/Mazel, 1978); Carolyn Winget, *Dimensions of Dreams* (Gainesville: University Presses of Florida, 1979); David Koulack, *To Catch a Dream* (Ithaca, N.Y.: State University of New York Press, 1991); Arthur Arkin et al., *The Mind in Sleep* (Hillsdale, N.J.: Lawrence Erlbaum Associates, 1978).

14. Daniel Halpern, ed., *Writers on Artists* (San Francisco: North Point Press, 1988), 102–3.

15. "Closing Messages of the Council, to Artists," in Walter M. Abbott, S.J., ed., *The Documents of Vatican II* (New York: Association Press, 1966), 732.

Conclusion

1. Brother Lawrence of the Resurrection, *The Practice of the Presence of God* (Westminster, Md.: Newman Press, 1957).

2. Jean-Pierre de Caussade, *Abandonment to Divine Providence* (Garden City, N.Y.: Doubleday Image Books, 1967).

3. The disease of leprosy is now called Hansen's disease. It is no longer considered contagious, and people with the disease are no longer confined to leprosariums.

Bibliography

Almond, Philip. *Mystical Experience and Religious Doctrine: An Investigation of the Study of Mysticism in World Religions.* Berlin and New York: Mouton, 1982.

Arintero, John G. *The Mystical Evolution in the Development Vitality of the Church.* 2 vols. St. Louis: Herder, 1950.

Bellah, Robert N. *The Broken Covenant: American Civil Religion in Time of Trial.* New York: Seabury, 1975.

Bellah, Robert N., et al. *Habits of the Heart.* New York: Harper and Row, 1985.

Boff, Leonardo. *St. Francis of Assisi: A Model for Human Liberation.* New York: Crossroad, 1982.

Bonner, Gerald. "The Spirituality of St. Augustine and Its Influence on Western Mysticism." *Sorbonost* 4 (1982).

Boorstin, Daniel J. *The Americans: The National Experience.* New York: Random House, 1965.

Bouyer, Louis. "Mysticism: An Essay on the History of the World." In *Understanding Mysticism,* ed. Richard Woods, 42–55. Garden City, N.Y.: Doubleday Image Books, 1980.

Bouyer, Louis, Jean Leclercq, and François Vandenbroucke. *A History of Christian Spirituality.* New York: Seabury, 1982. Vol. 1, *The Spirituality of the New Testament and the Fathers.* Vol. 2, *The Spirituality of the Middle Ages.*

Carr, Anne E. A. *A Search for Wisdom and Spirit: Thomas Merton's Theology of the Self.* Notre Dame, Ind.: University of Notre Dame Press, 1988.

Coleman, John A., S.J. *An American Strategic Theology.* New York: Paulist Press, 1982.

———. *One Hundred Years of Catholic Social Thought: Celebrations and Challenge.* Maryknoll, N.Y.: Orbis Books, 1991.

Colson, Chuck, and Jack Eckerd. *Why America Doesn't Work.* Dallas: Word Publishing, 1992.

Congar, Yves. *Lay People in the Church: A Study for a Theology of the Laity.* Westminster, Md.: Newman Press, 1965.

Cousins, Ewert. *Bonaventure and the Coincidence of Opposites.* Chicago: Franciscan Herald Press, 1978.

———. *Global Spirituality: Toward the Meeting of the Mystical Paths.* Madras: University of Madras, Radhakrishnan Institute for Advanced Study in Philosophy, 1985.

Desan, Wilfred. *Let the Future Come: Perspectives for a Planetary Peace.* Vol. 3. *The Planetary Man.* Washington, D.C.: Georgetown University Press, 1987.

de Tocqueville, Alexis. *Democracy in America.* Trans. George Lawrence, ed. J. P. Mayer. New York: Doubleday, 1969.

Diehl, William E. *The Monday Connection: A Spirituality of Competence, Affirmation, and a Support in the Workplace.* San Francisco: Harper San Francisco, 1991.

Dodds, E. R. *Pagan and Christian in an Age of Anxiety.* Cambridge University Press, 1965.

Droel, William L. *Business People: The Spirituality of Work.* Chicago: ACTA Publications, 1990.

Eliade, Mircea. *The Sacred and the Profane.* New York: Harcourt, Brace, Jovanovich, 1959.

———. *A History of Religious Ideas.* Vol. 3. Trans. Willard R. Trask. Chicago: University of Chicago Press, 1985.

Fitzmeyer, Joseph A., S.J. *A Christological Catechism.* New York: Paulist Press, 1991.

Flannery, Austin, O.P., ed. *Vatican Council II: The Conciliar and Post Conciliar Documents.* Grand Rapids, Mich.: William B. Eerdmans Publishing Co., 1992.

Fontaine, Jacques. "The Practice of Christian Life: The Birth of the Laity." In Bernard McGinn and John Meyendorff, eds. *Christian Spirituality: Origins to the Twelfth Century.* New York: Crossroad, 1986, 453–91.

Foster, Richard. *Money, Sex and Power: The Challenge of the Disciplined Life.* San Francisco: HarperSanFrancisco, 1985.

Frend, W. H. C. *Martyrdom and Persecution in the Early Church.* New York: Oxford, 1965.

———. *Martyrdom and Persecution: A Study of a Conflict from the Maccabees to Donatus.* New York: New York University Press, 1967.

Fowler, James. *Stages of Faith.* San Francisco: Harper and Row, 1981.

Green, Thomas H. *Darkness in the Marketplace: The Christian at Prayer in the World.* Notre Dame, Ind.: Ave Maria Press, 1981.

Gregson, Vernon J., Jr. *Lonergan: Spirituality and the Meeting of Religions*. Lanham, Md.: University Press of America, 1985.

Griffin, Emilie. *The Reflective Executive*. New York: Crossroad, 1993.

Guinness, Os. *Winning Back the Soul of American Business*. Washington, D.C.: Hourglass Publishers, 1990.

Haughey, John C. *Converting 9 to 5: A Spirituality of Daily Work*. New York: Crossroad, 1989.

———. *The Holy Use of Money: Personal Finances in Light of Christian Faith*. New York: Crossroad, 1989.

Hennelly, Alfred T. *Liberation Theology: A Documentary History*. Maryknoll, N.Y.: Orbis Books, 1990.

Hoge, Dean R. *Converts, Dropouts, Returnees: A Study of Religious Change among Catholics*. New York: Pilgrim Press, 1981.

Holland, Joe. *Creative Communion: Toward a Spirituality of Work*. Mahwah, N.J.: Paulist Press, 1989.

James, William. *The Varieties of Religious Experience: A Study in Human Nature*. New York: Collier-Macmillan, 1961.

Jung, C. G. *Modern Man in Search of a Soul*. New York: Harcourt Brace, 1933.

Kasper, Walter. *Jesus the Christ*. Ramsey, N.J.: Paulist Press, 1977.

Knowles, David. *The Nature of Mysticism*. New York: Hawthorne Books, 1966.

Krieg, Robert. *Story-Shaped Christology: The Role of Narratives in Identifying Jesus Christ*. Mahwah, N.J.: Paulist Press, 1988.

Levinson, Daniel J. *The Seasons of a Man's Life*. New York: Knopf, 1978.

Lonergan, Bernard J. F., S.J. *Method in Theology*. New York: Herder and Herder, 1972.

———. *Second Collection*. Ed. William J. Ryan, S.J., and Bernard J. Tyrrell, S.J. Philadelphia: Westminster, 1974.

McGinn, Bernard. *The Foundations of Mysticism*. Vol. 1. New York: Crossroad, 1992.

Merton, Thomas. *The Seven Storey Mountain*. New York: Harcourt, Brace and Co., 1948.

———. *Thoughts in Solitude*. New York: Farrar, Straus and Cudahy, 1958.

———. *Conjectures of a Guilty Bystander*. New York: Image Books, 1968.

———. *New Seeds of Contemplation*. New York: New Directions, 1972.

———. *Contemplation in a World of Action*. New York: Doubleday, 1973.

Neill, S. C., and H. R. Weber, eds. *The Layman in Christian History*. Philadelphia: Westminster, 1963.

O'Brien, David. *The Renewal of American Catholicism*. New York: Oxford University Press, 1972.

Peck, M. Scott. *The Road Less Traveled*. New York: Simon and Schuster, 1978.

Pierre, Gregory F. Augustine, ed. *Of Human Hands: A Reader in the Spirituality of Work*. Minneapolis: Augsburg, 1991; Chicago: ACTA Publications, 1991.

Pope, Marvin H. *Song of Songs: A New Translation with Introduction and Commentary*. Anchor Bible 7C. Garden City, N.Y.: Doubleday, 1977.

Rahner, Karl. *Theological Investigations*. Vol. 3. *Theology of the Spiritual Life*. Baltimore: Helicon Press, 1967.

————. *The Practice of Faith*. New York: Crossroad, 1983.

Reiser, William. *Talking about Jesus Today*. New York: Paulist Press, 1993.

Rosenberg, Joel. *Jewish Spirituality: From the Bible through the Middle Ages*. Ed. Arthur Gree. New York: Crossroad, 1986.

Segundo, Juan Luis. *The Liberation of Theology*. Maryknoll, N.Y.: Orbis Books, 1976.

Smart, Ninian. "Understanding Religious Experience." In *Mysticism and Religious Traditions*. Ed. Steven T. Katz, 10–21. New York: Oxford University Press, 1978.

Sobrino, Jon. *Christology at the Crossroads*. Maryknoll, N.Y.: Orbis Books, 1978.

Thompson, William M. *The Jesus Debate: A Survey and Synthesis*. Ramsey, N.J.: Paulist Press, 1985.

Underhill, Evelyn. *Practical Mysticism: A Little Book for Normal People*. New York: E. P. Dutton, 1915.

————. *Mysticism: A Study in the Nature and Development in Man's Spiritual Consciousness*. 12th ed. Cleveland and New York: World, 1965.

Veroff, Joseph, et al. *The Inner American: A Self-Portrait from 1957–1976*. New York: Basic Books, 1981.